A Note From Rick Renner

I am on a personal quest to see a "revival of the Bible" so people can establish their lives on a firm foundation that will stand strong and endure the test as the end-time storm winds begin to intensify.

In order to experience a revival of the Bible in your personal life, it is important to take time each day to read, receive, and apply its truths to your life. James tells us that if we will continue in the perfect law of liberty — refusing to be forgetful hearers but determined to be doers — we will be blessed in our ways. As you watch or listen to the programs in this series and work through this corresponding study guide, I trust that you will search the Scriptures and allow the Holy Spirit to help you hear something new from God's Word that applies specifically to your life. I encourage you to be a doer of the Word that He reveals to you. Whatever the cost, I assure you — it will be worth it.

Thy words were found, and I did eat them;
and thy word was unto me the joy and rejoicing of mine heart:
for I am called by thy name, O Lord God of hosts.
—Jeremiah 15:16

Your brother and friend in Jesus Christ,

Rick Renner

Rick Renner

Unless otherwise indicated, all scripture quotations are taken from the *King James Version* of the Bible.

Moses and the Ten Plagues

8316 E. 73rd St.
Tulsa, Oklahoma 74133

Published by Rick Renner Ministries
www.renner.org

ISBN 13: 978-1-6803-1871-5

eBook ISBN 13: 978-1-6803-1872-2

How To Use This Study Guide

This ten-lesson study guide corresponds to "***Moses and the Ten Plagues" With Rick Renner*** (Renner TV). Each lesson in this study guide covers a topic that is addressed during the program series, with questions and references supplied to draw you deeper into your own private study of the Scriptures on this subject.

To derive the most benefit from this study guide, consider the following:

First, watch or listen to the program prior to working through the corresponding lesson in this guide. (Programs can also be viewed at **renner.org** by clicking on the Media/Archives links.)

Second, take the time to look up the scriptures included in each lesson. Prayerfully consider their application to your own life.

Third, use a journal or notebook to make note of your answers to each lesson's Study Questions and Practical Application challenges.

Fourth, invest specific time in prayer and in the Word of God to consult with the Holy Spirit. Write down the scriptures or insights He reveals to you.

Finally, take action! Whatever the Lord tells you to do according to His Word, do it.

For added insights on this subject, it is recommended that you obtain Rick Renner's books ***How To Keep Your Head on Straight in a World Gone Crazy*** and ***Last-Days Survival Guide***. You may also select from Rick's other available resources by placing your order at **renner.org** or by calling 1-800-742-5593.

TOPIC

The Plight of Israel in Egypt

SCRIPTURES

1. **Exodus 1:6,7** — And Joseph died, and all his brethren, and all that generation. And the children of Israel were fruitful, and increased abundantly, and multiplied, and waxed exceeding mighty; and the land was filled with them.
2. **Genesis 47:27** — And Israel dwelt in the land of Egypt, in the country of Goshen; and they had possessions therein, and grew, and multiplied exceedingly.
3. **Exodus 1:8-22** — Now there arose up a new king over Egypt, which knew not Joseph. And he said unto his people, Behold, the people of the children of Israel are more and mightier than we: Come on, let us deal wisely with them; lest they multiply, and it come to pass, that, when there falleth out any war, they join also unto our enemies, and fight against us, and so get them up out of the land. Therefore they did set over them taskmasters to afflict them with their burdens. And they built for Pharaoh treasure cities, Pithom and Raamses. But the more they afflicted them, the more they multiplied and grew. And they were grieved because of the children of Israel. And the Egyptians made the children of Israel to serve with rigour: And they made their lives bitter with hard bondage, in morter, and in brick, and in all manner of service in the field: all their service, wherein they made them serve, was with rigour. And the king of Egypt spake to the Hebrew midwives, of which the name of the one was Shiphrah, and the name of the other Puah. And he said, When ye do the office of a midwife to the Hebrew women, and see them upon the stools; if it be a son, then ye shall kill him: but if it be a daughter, then she shall live. But the midwives feared God, and did not as the king of Egypt commanded them, but saved the men children alive. And the king of Egypt called for the midwives, and said unto them, Why have ye done this thing, and have saved the men children alive? And the midwives said unto Pharaoh, Because the Hebrew women are not as the Egyptian women; for they are lively, and are delivered ere the midwives come in

unto them. Therefore God dealt well with the midwives: and the people multiplied, and waxed very mighty. And it came to pass, because the midwives feared God, that he made them houses. And Pharaoh charged all his people, saying, Every son that is born ye shall cast into the river, and every daughter ye shall save alive.

4. **Isaiah 54:17** — No weapon that is formed against thee shall prosper….

GREEK WORDS

There are no Greek words in this lesson.

SYNOPSIS

The ten lessons in this study on ***Moses and the Ten Plagues*** will focus on the following topics:

- The Plight of Israel in Egypt
- The Birth of Moses
- The Call of God 'Wakes Up' in Moses
- The Encounter on Mount Horeb
- The Promise of God To Punish Egypt
- God Sends Moses to Pharaoh
- Plagues of Blood, Frogs, and Lice
- Plagues of Flies, Disease, and Boils
- Plagues of Hail and Locusts
- Darkness and the Death of the Firstborn

The emphasis of this lesson:

It is documented in Scripture as well as in secular records that the nation of Israel was at one time living in the land of Egypt. When Joseph brought them in, they were highly favored, but many years later, a new Pharaoh rose to power that enslaved the Israelites out of fear that they would turn against them.

What does the Winter Palace, which is a major part of the New Hermitage Museum, in Saint Petersburg, Russia, have in common with the nation of Egypt? The answer is *history*. In the basement of the Winter

Palace is an extraordinary collection of ancient artifacts from the land of Egypt. There are papyrus scrolls, caskets, coffins, and mummies dating back thousands of years. In fact, the relics one finds there are much like what one would find in the Egyptian museum located in downtown Cairo, Egypt.

Of all the objects found in the Museum of Cairo, one item stands out among them all. It's the remarkable, ancient stele that documents the fact that at one time the children of Israel did actually reside in Egypt. It confirms that the biblical events we read about in the book of Exodus are true. Their enslavement to the Egyptians and their miraculous deliverance by the hand of God through Moses really did take place — a fact also confirmed by Josephus, a First-Century Jewish historian.

What Do We Know About Josephus?

Josephus was noted as being the most authoritative and accurate historian of Jewish history that has ever lived. Initially, he served in the military and led Jewish forces against the Romans during the first Jewish-Roman War. After being defeated, Josephus surrendered to the Roman General Vespasian — the same person who decided to keep Josephus as his personal assistant and interpreter.

Without question, Josephus was found to be a faithful and brilliant assistant. When Vespasian later became Emperor, he granted Josephus freedom, and for that act of kindness, Josephus chose to assume the Emperor's family name *Flavius.* That is why he is called *Flavius Josephus.*

Of all of Josephus' works, his most important include the *Antiquities of the Jews*, which is a very comprehensive view of Jewish history from the time of Adam until the time of Christ. Today, Josephus' works are still considered to be the most accurate source next to the Bible for authenticating Jewish history. In fact, when scholars refer to Jewish history, they depend mostly on the works of Josephus because they are so comprehensive and authoritative. His accounts have even helped researchers understand and interpret the findings of modern-day excavations.

The Israelites Lived in Goshen

The book of Genesis ends with the children of Israel being saved from a severe worldwide famine. Joseph, who was the great grandson of the patriarch Abraham, used his divine gifting to interpret Pharaoh's dream, which was a message from God warning of a terrible famine that was coming. Pharaoh promoted Joseph to second in command of all of Egypt, and with great wisdom, Joseph developed and implemented a strategic plan that saved his family and the entire world from starvation.

Genesis 47:27 says, "And Israel dwelt in the land of Egypt, in the country of Goshen; and they had possessions therein, and grew, and multiplied exceedingly." The Bible says when Israel came into Egypt during Joseph's time, they settled in *Goshen* — which was the best land in Egypt. Goshen was located in the eastern delta of the River Nile in lower Egypt, which was well-watered and extremely fertile. Although the word "Goshen" is a mystery, it seems to mean "cultivated" or "luscious" and depicts a "prosperous" land.

The Israelites were treated *royally* because of Joseph's influence and that is why they were given lush lands in lower Egypt. There was a large city there called Avaris, which during the time of Rameses II (also known as Rameses the Great) was developed and re-named Pi-Ramesses. Some people call it Pithom and Rameses as it is referred to in Scripture. This was actually two cities — what we might call twin cities — and it was in this huge ancient metroplex that the children of Israel lived.

When the Bible says, "...They had possessions therein, and grew, and multiplied exceedingly" (Genesis 47:27), the word "possessions" depicts *financial prosperity*. The Israelites experienced great prosperity and became numerically huge. God had abundantly blessed them due to the supernatural favor on Joseph's life.

The Children of Israel Were Originally Called *Canaanites*, *Shepherd Kings*, and *Asiatics*

The book of Exodus picks up where Genesis leaves off. It says, "And Joseph died, and all his brethren, and all that generation. And the children of Israel were fruitful, and increased abundantly, and multiplied, and waxed exceeding mighty; and the land was filled with them (Exodus 1:6,7).

It's interesting to note that many modern historians say there is no evidence that the children of Israel were ever in the land of Egypt. However, at that time in history, the children of Israel were called *Canaanites*, *shepherd kings*, and *Asiatics*. This is how they're classified in Egyptian writings. There is actually only one known Egyptian record in which the descendants of Abraham are called the children of Israel, and it's found etched on a stele (or stone tablet) that presently resides in the Cairo Egyptian Museum.

What happened after Joseph's death? The Bible says, "Now there arose up a new king over Egypt, which knew not Joseph" (Exodus 1:8). About 60 years after the death of Joseph a revolution took place. At that time, upper and lower Egypt were united into one kingdom, and a new Pharaoh came into power who did not appreciate Joseph's monumental contributions and regarded the Canaanites (Israelites) with scorn.

The birth and early years of Moses — which began 80 years before the Exodus — possibly belong to the reigns of the Thutmose I and II. What's most interesting is that the mummified body of Thutmose II, which can be seen in the Cairo Museum, is covered with scabs. It's the only Pharaoh corpse to have such markings. This may be physical evidence of the boil plague that God sent upon Egypt. Moreover, some historians allege Thutmose I was the Pharaoh at the time of Moses' birth. If so, he would have been the pharaoh "which knew not Joseph" (Exodus 1:8) and began treating the Israelites with great contempt.

The 'New Pharaoh' Enslaved Israel Out of Fear

The Bible goes on to say, "And he (Pharaoh) said unto his people, Behold, the people of the children of Israel are more and mightier than we: Come on, let us deal wisely with them; lest they multiply, and it come to pass, that, when there falleth out any war, they join also unto our enemies, and fight against us, and so get them up out of the land" (Exodus 1:9,10).

History documents that Egyptians were famous for their sense of racial superiority. They feared invasions from the Hittites who lived just to their north and were regularly at war with them. If the people of Israel joined forces with the Hittites, it would pose a major threat to Egypt. This is what Pharaoh and the Egyptians greatly feared. Additionally, the Hebrews were important to the economy and infrastructure of Egypt.

So to clamp down and tighten his control on the children of Israel, Pharaoh said, "...Come on, let us deal wisely with them; lest they multiply..." (Exodus 1:10). The words "lest they multiply" indicate Pharaoh's efforts to curtail the Jewish birthrate. This is the first act of antisemitism recorded in Scripture. The Bible says, "Therefore they did set over them taskmasters to afflict them with their burdens. And they built for Pharaoh treasure cities, Pithom and Raamses" (Exodus 1:11).

Israel rose to great prosperity due to Joseph's influence. This prosperity was viewed with jealousy by many in Egypt. Out of this jealousy, the children of Israel were forced into hard labor and made to build many of the great cities and monuments in Egypt. There are paintings that show these "taskmasters" referred to in Exodus 1:11 armed with whips and rods. Taskmasters in the ancient world used "rods" to beat people into submission to work harder.

It's likely that the children of Israel were involved in building Pharaoh's "treasure cities" of Pithom and Rameses (Pi-Ramesses) on the ancient site of Avaris. Eventually, the city of Avaris was absorbed into the new city of Pi-Ramesses that was developed by Rameses II (the Great). Again, Pithom and Rameses were twin cities that became known as Pi-Ramesses — one of the greatest metroplexes in Egypt at that time. But eventually Israel became oppressed there.

Pharaoh's Harsh Treatment Prompted God's Multiplied Blessings on Israel

In spite of Pharaoh's harsh treatment, God continued to bless the children of Israel. Scripture says, "But the more they afflicted them, the more they multiplied and grew. And they were grieved because of the children of Israel" (Exodus 1:12). The word "grieved" here means to be "disgusted." This played into the Egyptian feeling of racial superiority. They believed they were better than everyone else and became thoroughly disgusted with the Hebrews that were multiplying among them.

The Egyptian's attitude moved from *fear* to *hatred* and then to *disgust*. The Bible says, "And the Egyptians made the children of Israel to serve with rigour: And they made their lives bitter with hard bondage, in morter, and in brick, and in all manner of service in the field: all their service, wherein they made them serve, was with rigour" (Exodus 1:13,14).

If you take a cruise up the Nile River today and stop at the different sites along the way, you'll see the ruins of massive brick buildings still standing from the period when the Israelites were enslaved in Egypt and they were forced to build using bricks. Egyptian bricks were baked in the sun and used in upper and lower Egypt for public and private buildings. It's worth noting that there are more bricks discovered bearing the name of Thutmose (the Pharaoh family during the time of Israel's bondage) than any other from that period.

Make no mistake: The Egyptians tried their best to break and eradicate the Israelites. This was the first recorded act of antisemitism. The ultimate purpose was the liquidation of the Hebrew race — but it didn't work. Instead, the nation of Israel flourished. Jewish historian Josephus noted these things saying:

> Now it happened that the Egyptians grew delicate and lazy, as to pains-taking; and gave themselves up to other pleasures, and in particular to the love of gain. They also became very ill-affected towards the Hebrews, as touched with envy at their prosperity. For when they saw how the nation of the Israelites flourished, and were become eminent already in plenty of wealth, which they had acquired by their virtue, and natural love of labor, they thought their increase was to their own detriment. And having in length of time forgotten the benefits they had received from Joseph; particularly the crown being now come into another family; they became very abusive to the Israelites; and contrived many ways of afflicting them: for they enjoined them to cut a great number of channels for the river, and to build walls for their cities, and ramparts... and by all this wore them out, and forced them to learn all sorts of mechanical arts, and to accustom themselves to hard labor... the Egyptians desired to destroy the Israelites by these labors....[1]

Friend, God will always take care of His people — *always*. In the midst of great affliction and hardship, the Bible records that the Israelites prospered, proving God's promise that *no weapon formed against us shall prosper* (*see* Isaiah 54:17).

Pharaoh Ordered the Death of Every Male Hebrew Baby

As envy and jealousy mounted, the Bible says, "And the king of Egypt spake to the Hebrew midwives, of which the name of the one was Shiphrah, and the name of the other Puah: And he said, When ye do the office of a midwife to the Hebrew women, and see them upon the stools;

if it be a son, then ye shall kill him: but if it be a daughter, then she shall live" (Exodus 1:15,16).

The key to understanding this passage is in knowing what these "stools" were. When the Hebrew women were in labor and ready to give birth to their babies, they would sit on stools by the river side. Once their infants were born, they were washed in the waters of the Nile. The king's order was that when the Hebrew baby boys were born, they were to be taken to the river and drowned. The baby girls were to be kept alive and assimilated into the Egyptian population.

Josephus also wrote about this, saying:

> One of those sacred Scribes, who are very sagacious in foretelling future events truly, told the King, that about this time there would a child be born to the Israelites, who, if he were reared, would bring the Egyptian dominion low; and would raise the Israelites: that he would excel all men in virtue; and obtain a glory that would be remembered through all ages. Which thing was so feared by the King, that, according to this man's opinion, he commanded that they should cast every male child, which was born to the Israelites, into the river, and destroy it....[2]

So Josephus tells us there was a prophecy that had been spoken about a Jewish deliverer — a male child — that would be born that would bring Egypt low and elevate the nation of Israel, and Pharaoh believed it. That is why he commanded the midwives to kill the Hebrew boys as they were born. Josephus added:

> ...Besides this, the Egyptian midwives should watch the labors of the Hebrew women, and observe what is born... he enjoined also, that if any parents should disobey him, and venture to save their male children alive, they and their families should be destroyed.
>
> This was a severe affliction indeed to those that suffered it: not only as they were deprived of their sons; and while they were the parents themselves, they were obliged to be subservient to the destruction of their own children, but as it was to be supposed to tend to the extermination of their nation....[3]

The Midwives Refused To Obey Pharaoh's Murderous Command

How did the midwives respond to Pharaoh's demands? Exodus 1:17, says, "But the midwives feared God, and did *not* as the king of Egypt commanded them, but saved the men children alive." Although the midwives feared Pharaoh, they feared God more. Therefore, they chose to obey God rather than men.

Greatly angered by their actions, the Bible says, "And the king of Egypt called for the midwives, and said unto them, Why have ye done this thing, and have saved the men children alive? And the midwives said unto Pharaoh, Because the Hebrew women are not as the Egyptian women; for they are lively, and are delivered ere the midwives come in unto them" (Exodus 1:18,19). Many have looked at this verse and thought the midwives lied, but that is not the case. They told the truth. The Hebrew women were more robust than Egyptian women, giving birth to their babies much faster.

Exodus 1:20 and 21 goes on to say, "Therefore God dealt well with the midwives: and the people multiplied, and waxed very mighty. And it came to pass, because the midwives feared God, that he made them houses." God blessed the midwives for their bravery to obey Him rather than man. Although they normally had no children of their own, God enabled them to have children and establish a flourishing family. The worse the persecution became, the more God blessed them.

You can trust that God will do the same thing for you! As you obediently follow Him — even if the enemy tries to oppress and destroy you — God has decreed that *no weapon formed against you shall prosper* (*see* Isaiah 54:17).

In our next lesson, we will continue our study and focus on the birth of Moses and how God raised up the prophesied deliverer right under Pharaoh's nose.

STUDY QUESTIONS

Study to shew thyself approved unto God, a workman that needeth not to be ashamed, rightly dividing the word of truth.
— 2 Timothy 2:15

1. Before you began this study, had you ever heard of *Flavius Josephus*? What new insights did you learn about this renowned historian? How about the land of Goshen?
2. According to Scripture, Joseph — Abraham's great grandson — brought his family to live in Egypt to escape the severe famine. How many people does Genesis 46:26,27 say originally went down to live in Egypt? Not counting women and children, approximately how many left Egypt at the time of the Exodus (*see* Numbers 1:45,46)?
3. History records that the Egyptians lived with a proud feeling of racial superiority. What does Proverbs 11:2 and 16:18 say happens when we operate in *pride*? How about *humility*? (*See* Proverbs 22:4; 29:23.)

PRACTICAL APPLICATION

But be ye doers of the word, and not hearers only, deceiving your own selves.
—James 1:22

1. If you had been one of the midwives or a parent who was commanded by the king of Egypt to destroy your baby boy, how do you think you would have responded? How does the Lord's response to the midwives encourage you to obey God rather than man?
2. Out of deep-seated fear, the new Pharaoh that arose enslaved the children of Israel in an attempt to control them and to stop them from multiplying. Pause and pray: *Lord, is there an area of my life where I'm being driven by fear and I'm trying to control people (or things)? If so, where? What am I afraid of? What do I need to do differently in this area to bring You glory and see things improve?*

---

[1] Flavius Josephus, "The Words of Flavius Josephus: Translated by William Whiston; Antiquities of the Jews," Book II, chap. 9.1.

[2] Flavius Josephus, "The Words of Flavius Josephus: Translated by William Whiston; Antiquities of the Jews," Book II, chap. 9.2.

[3] Flavius Josephus, "The Words of Flavius Josephus: Translated by William Whiston; Antiquities of the Jews," Book II, chap. 9.2.

TOPIC
The Birth of Moses

SCRIPTURES

1. **Exodus 1:13-22** — And the Egyptians made the children of Israel to serve with rigour: And they made their lives bitter with hard bondage, in morter, and in brick, and in all manner of service in the field: all their service, wherein they made them serve, was with rigour. And the king of Egypt spake to the Hebrew midwives, of which the name of the one was Shiphrah, and the name of the other Puah. And he said, When ye do the office of a midwife to the Hebrew women, and see them upon the stools; if it be a son, then ye shall kill him: but if it be a daughter, then she shall live. But the midwives feared God, and did not as the king of Egypt commanded them, but saved the men children alive. And the king of Egypt called for the midwives, and said unto them, Why have ye done this thing, and have saved the men children alive? And the midwives said unto Pharaoh, Because the Hebrew women are not as the Egyptian women; for they are lively, and are delivered ere the midwives come in unto them. Therefore God dealt well with the midwives: and the people multiplied, and waxed very mighty. And it came to pass, because the midwives feared God, that he made them houses. And Pharaoh charged all his people, saying, Every son that is born ye shall cast into the river, and every daughter ye shall save alive.
2. **Exodus 2:1-10** — And there went a man of the house of Levi, and took to wife a daughter of Levi. And the woman conceived, and bare a son: and when she saw him that he was a goodly child, she hid him three months. And when she could not longer hide him, she took for him an ark of bulrushes, and daubed it with slime and with pitch, and put the child therein; and she laid it in the flags by the river's brink. And his sister stood afar off, to wit what would be done to him. And the daughter of Pharaoh came down to wash herself at the river; and her maidens walked along by the river's side; and when she saw the ark among the flags, she sent her maid to fetch it. And when she had opened it, she saw the child: and, behold, the babe wept. And she had

compassion on him, and said, This is one of the Hebrews' children. Then said his sister to Pharaoh's daughter, Shall I go and call to thee a nurse of the Hebrew women, that she may nurse the child for thee? And Pharaoh's daughter said to her, Go. And the maid went and called the child's mother. And Pharaoh's daughter said unto her, Take this child away, and nurse it for me, and I will give thee thy wages. And the woman took the child, and nursed it. And the child grew, and she brought him unto Pharaoh's daughter, and he became her son. And she called his name Moses....

3. **Hebrews 11:23** — By faith Moses, when he was born, was hid three months of his parents, because they saw he was a proper child; and they were not afraid of the king's commandment.
4. **Acts 7:20** — In which time Moses was born, and was exceeding fair, and nourished up in his father's house three months.
5. **Proverbs 22:6** — Train up a child in the way he should go: and when he is old, he will not depart from it.
6. **Acts 7:21,22** — And when he was cast out, Pharaoh's daughter took him up, and nourished him for her own son. And Moses was learned in all the wisdom of the Egyptians, and was mighty in words and in deeds.

GREEK WORDS

1. "proper child" — **ἀστεῖος** (*asteios*): polished; elegant; unusual
2. "exceeding fair" — **ἀστεῖος** (*asteios*): polished; elegant; unusual
3. "nourished" — **ἀνατρέφω** (*anatrepho*): rear; nourish; educate; train
4. "for" — **εἰς** (*eis*): into, indicating transition
5. "learned" — **παιδεύω** (*paideuo*): instructed; educated; trained; he reached his full potential as an Egyptian man
6. "all" — **πάσῃ** (*pase*): all, an all-inclusive term
7. "wisdom" — **σοφία** (*sophia*): insight, skill, intelligence, philosophy, sophistication; especially bright, educated, astute, smart, or eminently enlightened.

SYNOPSIS

The New Hermitage Museum, which includes the extravagant Winter Palace, is located in Saint Petersburg, Russia, and it is filled with room after room of remarkable treasures from around the world. For instance, there is a room called the Jupiter Room, and it was designed particularly to house Greek and Roman statues from the ancient world. Amongst these statues is a sculpture of the god Jupiter that dates back to the First Century.

Another amazing room to explore at the Hermitage is the Egyptian Room, and it contains rare and priceless relics from virtually every period of Egypt's history. These include ancient papyrus scrolls, original steles, mummies, and sarcophagi, which are coffins and caskets. This room's contents are very similar to what one would find in the city of Cairo, Egypt — especially as one journeyed into the heart of the Great Pyramid of Giza.

The Egyptian dynasty is no fairy tale and neither is their enslavement of the nation of Israel, which is documented in Egypt's history. The fact is, Moses was a real historical figure that God raised up to deliver the Hebrew nation out of Egyptian bondage. His birth and the events surrounding it are detailed in several places in Scripture, and that will be the focus of this lesson.

The emphasis of this lesson:

The Bible says Moses was unique and exceedingly fair as a child, and his parents took remarkable care of him. After God divinely orchestrated Moses' rescue from the Nile by Pharaoh's daughter, He made a way for the infant to be nursed and nurtured in the ways of God by his birth mother in his most formative years.

A REVIEW OF LESSON 1

The Egyptians Forced Israel Into Hard Labor

As we noted in our first lesson, the descendants of Abraham were awarded the best land in the country of Egypt — the land of Goshen — as a result of Joseph's monumental contributions to save Egypt during a severe famine. But after Joseph died, a new Pharaoh arose that didn't know or appreciate what Joseph had done. The Bible says that out of great fear, "… The Egyptians made the children of Israel to serve with rigour: And they made their lives bitter with hard bondage, in morter, and in brick, and in all manner of service in the field: all their service, wherein they made them serve, was with rigour" (Exodus 1:13,14).

To maintain a tight rein of control over the children of Israel, taskmasters were placed over them that beat them into submission with rods and forced them into grueling, hard labor. Specifically, the Egyptians made the Israelites build the twin treasure cities of Pharaoh. These were the cities of Pithom and Rameses, which became known as Pi-Ramesses, and were constructed of bricks made of clay and straw formed by the hands of the Israelites. All kinds of buildings — public and private — were made of these bricks and erected in places up and down the Nile River, the remnants of which can still be seen today.

Pharaoh Ordered Every Male Hebrew Baby To Be Killed

As the children of Israel continued to multiply, the Bible says, "And the king of Egypt spake to the Hebrew midwives, of which the name of the one was Shiphrah, and the name of the other Puah: And he said, When ye do the office of a midwife to the Hebrew women, and see them upon the stools; if it be a son, then ye shall kill him: but if it be a daughter, then she shall live" (Exodus 1:15,16).

As we learned in Lesson 1, when the Hebrew women were in labor and ready to give birth to their babies, they would sit on *stools* by the Nile River, and once their infants were born, they washed them in the river's waters. Pharaoh ordered that when the Hebrew baby boys were born, they were to be taken to the river and drowned. In contrast, the baby girls were to be kept alive and assimilated into the Egyptian population.

What motivated Pharaoh to decree such a hideous order of extermination? Jewish historian Josephus adds this insight:

> One of those sacred Scribes, who are very sagacious in foretelling future events truly, told the King, that about this time there would a child be born to the Israelites, who, if he were reared, would bring the Egyptian dominion low; and would raise the Israelites: that he would excel all men in virtue; and obtain a glory that would be remembered through all ages. Which thing was so feared by the King, that, according to this man's opinion, he commanded that they should cast every male child, which was born to the Israelites, into the river, and destroy it....[1]

Thus, there was a general belief that a Jewish deliverer — a male child — would be born to the Israelites that would bring Egypt low and exalt the nation of Israel. Pharaoh believed this prophecy, which is why he commanded the midwives to kill the Hebrew boys as they were born. Josephus added:

> ...Besides this, the Egyptian midwives should watch the labors of the Hebrew women, and observe what is born... he enjoined also, that if any parents should disobey him, and venture to save their male children alive, they and their families should be destroyed.
>
> This was a severe affliction indeed to those that suffered it: not only as they were deprived of their sons; and while they were the parents themselves, they were obliged to be subservient to the destruction of their own children, but as it was to be supposed to tend to the extermination of their nation....[2]

Here we see a vivid picture of Satan's hatred of the Jewish people — a hatred that has manifested again and again throughout the ages since the beginning of time. It is the first record of antisemitism recorded in Scripture.

The Midwives Feared God More Than Pharaoh

Exodus 1:17, says, "But the midwives feared God, and did not as the king of Egypt commanded them, but saved the men children alive." Although the midwives feared Pharaoh, they feared God more. Hence, they chose to obey God rather than men.

Infuriated for not carrying out his orders, the Bible says, "And the king of Egypt called for the midwives, and said unto them, Why have ye done this thing, and have saved the men children alive? And the midwives said unto Pharaoh, Because the Hebrew women are not as the Egyptian women; for they are lively, and are delivered ere the midwives come in unto them" (Exodus 1:18,19). Although it may seem the midwives lied, there was truth in what they said. The Hebrew women were more robust than Egyptian women and gave birth to their babies much faster.

God Rewarded the Midwives' Obedience

Because they feared God more than man, the Bible says, "Therefore God dealt well with the midwives: and the people multiplied, and waxed very mighty. And it came to pass, because the midwives feared God, that he made them houses" (Exodus 1:20,21). Obedience opened the door to God's blessings on the midwives. God enabled them to have their own children and establish a flourishing family.

Needless to say, Pharaoh was enraged that the Hebrew males were being permitted to live. Exodus 1:22 tells us, "And Pharaoh charged all his people, saying, Every son that is born ye shall cast into the river, and every daughter ye shall save alive."

It's important to note that the Egyptians believed the Nile River was the birth place of the gods. So the order to drown the Hebrew boys was not just an act of murder — it was a sacrifice to the gods of the River Nile.

Interestingly, as Egypt increased the pressure and persecution on Israel, God increased His blessings on them. And since God is no respecter of persons, you can trust that He will do the same thing for you! As you obey what He has told you to do, God has decreed that *no weapon formed against you shall prosper* (*see* Isaiah 54:17).

Moses' Parents Were Remarkable

The second chapter of Exodus begins by introducing us to Moses' parents. The Bible says, "And there went a man of the house of Levi, and took to wife a daughter of Levi. And the woman conceived, and bare a son: and when she saw him that he was a goodly child, she hid him three months" (Exodus 2:1,2). According to Exodus 6:20, the name of this man was Amram, and the woman he took to be his wife was Jochebed.

This unique couple is actually talked about in a few different places in Scripture, including Hebrews 11:23, which says, "By faith Moses, when he was born, was hid three months of his parents, because they saw he was a proper child; and they were not afraid of the king's commandment." Note the words "proper child." This is a translation of the Greek word *asteios*, which means *polished*; *elegant*; *unusual*, or *sophisticated*. The moment Moses was born, his parents could clearly see there was something unusual and special about him.

This fact is echoed by Stephen in Acts 7:20, which says, "In which time Moses was born, and was exceeding fair, and nourished up in his father's house three months." The words "exceeding fair" are once again a translation of the Greek word *asteios*, meaning *polished*; *elegant*; or *unusual.*

Even though Pharaoh had commanded that every Hebrew male child born was to be killed, Moses' parents were not afraid of his command. They had a word from God about this child that had been given to Amram in a dream. This is spoken to us clearly in the writings of Josephus:

> Amram awaked, and told it to Jochebed, who was his wife... and they nourished the child at home privately for three months. But after that time Amram, fearing he should be discovered; and by falling under the King's displeasure both he and his child should perish; and so he should make the promise of God of none effect; he determined rather to entrust the safety and care of the child to God, than to depend on his own concealment of him, which he looked upon as a thing uncertain; and whereby both the child, so privately to be nourished, and himself, would be in imminent danger. But he believed that God would some way for certain procure the safety of the child....[3]

So we see Moses referred to as a "proper child" in Hebrew 11:23, "exceeding fair" in Acts 7:20, and a "goodly child" in Exodus 2:2. It's also interesting to note that Moses was *not* the firstborn of the family. Scripture says he had an older brother named Aaron and a sister named Miriam, so he had at least two older siblings.

Like Noah, Moses Found Safety in an 'Ark'

The Bible goes on to say, "And when she [Jochebed] could not longer hide him, she took for him an ark of bulrushes, and daubed it with slime and with pitch, and put the child therein; and she laid it in the flags by the river's brink" (Exodus 2:3). Isn't it interesting that Moses' mother made an "ark" of bulrushes. The word "ark" here is the same word used for the "ark" that Noah built hundreds of years earlier. Undoubtedly, Jochebed and Amram had heard and knew the account of Noah's ark, and she fashioned the ark of bulrushes for Moses, believing it to be an "ark of deliverance" for her son and the nation of Israel. When Moses' mother let go of that boat, she released something precious, believing that God would take care of her son and perhaps even find a way to give him back to her.

With regard to the tiny ark and its placement upon the waters, Josephus shared these insights:

> ...They made an ark of bulrushes, after the manner of a cradle, and of a bigness sufficient for an infant to be laid in, without being too straitened. They then daubed it over with slime, which would naturally keep out the water... and put the infant into it; and setting it afloat upon the river, they left its preservation to God: so the river received the child, and carried him along. But Miriam, the child's sister, passed along upon the bank over against him, as her mother had bid her, to see whither the ark would be carried.[4]

This is exactly what we read in Exodus 2:4, which says, "And his sister stood afar off, to wit what would be done to him." The Bible continues by saying, "And the daughter of Pharaoh came down to wash herself at the river; and her maidens walked along by the river's side; and when she saw the ark among the flags, she sent her maid to fetch it. And when she had opened it, she saw the child: and, behold, the babe wept. And she had compassion on him, and said, This is one of the Hebrews' children" (Exodus 2:5,6).

Pharaoh's Daughter Rescued Moses From Her Father's Deadly Decree

As you read these verses, keep in mind that the Egyptians — which includes the Pharaoh's daughter — believed that the Nile River was the birthplace of the gods. Therefore, in the eyes of Pharaoh's daughter, it appeared as though the Nile was producing a new god. Even though she had been trained up to believe that the Hebrews were a people to be disdained, the cries of Moses melted the hardness of her heart. God had directed the current of the Nile to bring the baby right to Pharaoh's daughter in order to further His plan and carry out His purpose.

The historian Josephus weighed in on this as well saying:

> ...The King's daughter... was now diverting herself by the banks of the river: and seeing a cradle born along by the current, she sent some that could swim, and bid them bring the cradle to her. When those that were sent on this errand came to her with the cradle, and she saw the little child, she was greatly in love with it, on account of its largeness and beauty: for God had taken such great care in the formation of Moses, that he caused him to be thought worthy of bringing up and provided for by all those that

> had taken the most fatal resolutions, on account of the dread of his nativity, for the destruction of the rest of the Hebrew nation.[5]

Yet Moses' Birth Mother Raised Him in His Most Formative Years

This brings us to the fascinating turn of events recorded in Exodus 2:7-9, which says, "Then said his sister (Miriam) to Pharaoh's daughter, Shall I go and call to thee a nurse of the Hebrew women, that she may nurse the child for thee? And Pharaoh's daughter said to her, Go. And the maid went and called the child's mother. And Pharaoh's daughter said unto her, Take this child away, and nurse it for me, and I will give thee thy wages. And the woman took the child, and nursed it."

Josephus commented on this surprising — yet God-ordained — situation:

> Now Miriam was by when this happened… and she said, 'It is in vain that thou, O Queen, callest for these women for the nourishing of the child, who are no way of kin to it. But still, if thou wilt order one of the Hebrew women to be brought, perhaps it may admit the breast of one of its own nation.' Now, since she seemed to speak well… (Pharaoh's daughter) bid her procure such a one, and to bring one of those Hebrew women that gave suck. So when she had such authority given her, she came back, and brought the mother, who was known to no body there. And now the child gladly admitted the breast… and so it was that at the Queen's desire the nursing of the child was entirely intrusted to the mother.[6]

Apparently, God's plan was for Moses' mother to train him in his early, formative years — and be paid for it! No one but God Himself could have enabled Jochebed, Moses' mother, to rear her own son in the midst of Pharaoh's extermination edict. This means Moses' most impressionable years were spent with his mother who did not waste a moment to instill truth into him at that early age.

Proverbs 22:6 tells us, "Train up a child in the way he should go: and when he is old, he will not depart from it." What Jochebed planted in the fertile soil of Moses' soul stayed with him all through his life. Although it seemed to be inactive for many years, later on, at just the right time, those godly words of instruction came alive again.

What Does the Name 'Moses' Mean?

Exodus 2:10 goes on to say, "And the child grew, and she brought him unto Pharaoh's daughter, and he became her son. And she (Pharaoh's daughter) called his name Moses...."

To be clear, the name "Moses" is not a Hebrew name. It is a very Egyptian name, and it is derived from the name "Thutmose" — the name of the Pharaoh's family that was currently ruling. History reveals that there were many Egyptian Pharaohs whose name was Thutmose, and it means "son of Thoth." It is composed of the name of the Egyptian god *Thoth* combined with the word meaning to "be born." When the two parts are joined together, it means *one born of the god Thoth.*

Thoth was the Egyptian god of writing, magic, wisdom, sophistication, and development. It was believed that Thoth was said to be self-created, self-existing, and self-sufficient. This gives us greater understanding into why God introduced Himself to Moses as I AM THAT I AM. This revelation God gave to Moses was a declaration that God is the real self-existing, All-Sufficient One.

Once Pharaoh's daughter received Moses back into her home, the Bible says, "...Pharaoh's daughter took him up, and nourished him for her own son" (Acts 7:21). The word "nourished" in this verse is the Greek word *anatrepho*, which means *to rear*; *to nourish*; *to educate*; or *to train.* Interestingly, even the word "for" has significance. It is the Greek word *eis*, meaning *into*, which indicates *transition.* This word *eis* carries the idea of *movement* and points to the fact that Pharaoh's daughter was positioning Moses to become her own son and eventually the inheritor of the throne of Egypt. Josephus confirmed this in his writings, saying that Moses was heir to the throne of Egypt.

The Bible goes on to say, "And Moses was learned in all the wisdom of the Egyptians, and was mighty in words and in deeds" (Acts 7:22). In this verse, the word "learned" is the Greek word *paideuo*, which means *instructed*; *educated*; or *trained.* It conveys the idea that Moses had reached his *full potential* as an Egyptian man, having acquired all the wisdom and skill of the Egyptians.

The word "all" in Greek is the term *pase*, which means *all*, and is an *all-inclusive* term. And the word "wisdom" is a translation of the Greek word *sophia*, meaning *insight*, *skill*, *intelligence*, *philosophy*, and *sophistication.*

It can also indicate *one who is especially bright, educated, astute, smart, or eminently enlightened.*

Despite all of Moses' extensive Egyptian education and training, God had different plans for him. All the truth that his mother had instilled within him in his formidable years would eventually wake up within him when he became aware of the call of God on his life. This would take place suddenly when Moses reached the age of 40.

Friend, when you "Train up a child in the way he should go…when he is old, he will not depart from it" (Proverbs 22:6). This is God's promise to you concerning your children and your grandchildren. The seeds of truth you plant and water in them when they are little will eventually produce a harvest of good fruit when they are older. You have God's Word on it!

In our next lesson, we will look at how and when the call of God woke up in Moses.

STUDY QUESTIONS

Study to shew thyself approved unto God, a workman that needeth not to be ashamed, rightly dividing the word of truth.
— 2 Timothy 2:15

1. We can see from Scripture that Moses' parents were quite remarkable. How has this lesson expanded your understanding of their character and care for Moses? What new facts did you learn about Moses as an infant?
2. Proverbs 22:6 tells us, "Train up a child in the way he should go: and when he is old, he will not depart from it." Are you honoring this instruction from God? If so, how? What other ways might you use to teach and train your children and grandchildren in the ways of the Lord? (Consider Psalm 78:1-7; Deuteronomy 6:1-9.)

PRACTICAL APPLICATION

But be ye doers of the word, and not hearers only, deceiving your own selves.
—James 1:22

1. Obedience opened the door to God's blessings on the midwives. Can you recall a time when you obeyed what God asked you to do, and He blessed you in response? If so, briefly describe what took place.
2. When Jochebed, Moses' mother, let go of the tiny ark containing her son, she released something precious, believing God would take care of him. Is there someone or something you need to totally release into God's hands? *Who* or *what* do you need to entrust to God?
3. Acts 7:22 tells us that Moses reached his full potential as an Egyptian man and acquired all the wisdom and skill of the Egyptians. How do you think this in-depth education and training might have helped Moses when he became the leader of Israel and led them out of bondage?

---

[1] Flavius Josephus, "The Words of Flavius Josephus: Translated by William Whiston; Antiquities of the Jews," Book II, chap. 9.2.

[2] Flavius Josephus, "The Words of Flavius Josephus: Translated by William Whiston; Antiquities of the Jews," Book II, chap. 9.2.

[3] Flavius Josephus, "The Words of Flavius Josephus: Translated by William Whiston; Antiquities of the Jews," Book II, chap. 9.4.

[4] Flavius Josephus, "The Words of Flavius Josephus: Translated by William Whiston; Antiquities of the Jews," Book II, chap. 9.4.

[5] Flavius Josephus, "The Words of Flavius Josephus: Translated by William Whiston; Antiquities of the Jews," Book II, chap. 9.5.

[6] Flavius Josephus, "The Words of Flavius Josephus: Translated by William Whiston; Antiquities of the Jews," Book II, chap. 9.5.

LESSON 3

TOPIC

The Call of God 'Wakes Up' in Moses

SCRIPTURES

1. **Exodus 2:1-10** — And there went a man of the house of Levi, and took to wife a daughter of Levi. And the woman conceived, and bare

a son: and when she saw him that he was a goodly child, she hid him three months. And when she could not longer hide him, she took for him an ark of bulrushes, and daubed it with slime and with pitch, and put the child therein; and she laid it in the flags by the river's brink. And his sister stood afar off, to wit what would be done to him. And the daughter of Pharaoh came down to wash herself at the river; and her maidens walked along by the river's side; and when she saw the ark among the flags, she sent her maid to fetch it. And when she had opened it, she saw the child: and, behold, the babe wept. And she had compassion on him, and said, This is one of the Hebrews' children. Then said his sister to Pharaoh's daughter, Shall I go and call to thee a nurse of the Hebrew women, that she may nurse the child for thee? And Pharaoh's daughter said to her, Go. And the maid went and called the child's mother. And Pharaoh's daughter said unto her, Take this child away, and nurse it for me, and I will give thee thy wages. And the woman took the child, and nursed it. And the child grew, and she brought him unto Pharaoh's daughter, and he became her son. And she called his name Moses: and she said, Because I drew him out of the water.

2. **Acts 7:21-23** — And when he was cast out, Pharaoh's daughter took him up, and nourished him for her own son. And Moses was learned in all the wisdom of the Egyptians, and was mighty in words and in deeds. And when he was full forty years old, it came into his heart to visit his brethren the children of Israel.
3. **Proverbs 22:6** — Train up a child in the way he should go: and when he is old, he will not depart from it.
4. **Exodus 2:11,12,15-19** — And it came to pass in those days, when Moses was grown, that he went out unto his brethren, and looked on their burdens: and he spied an Egyptian smiting an Hebrew, one of his brethren. And he looked this way and that way, and when he saw that there was no man, he slew the Egyptian, and hid him in the sand.... Now when Pharaoh heard this thing, he sought to slay Moses. But Moses fled from the face of Pharaoh, and dwelt in the land of Midian: and he sat down by a well. Now the priest of Midian had seven daughters: and they came and drew water, and filled the troughs to water their father's flock. And the shepherds came and drove them away: but Moses stood up and helped them, and watered their flock. And when they came to Reuel their father, he said, How is it that ye are come so soon to day? And they said, An Egyptian delivered us out

of the hand of the shepherds, and also drew water enough for us, and watered the flock.

5. **Exodus 2:24,25** — And God heard their groaning, and God remembered his covenant with Abraham, with Isaac, and with Jacob. And God looked upon the children of Israel, and God had respect unto them.

GREEK WORDS

1. "nourished" — **ἀνατρέφω** (*anatrepho*): rear; nourish; educate; train
2. "for" — **εἰς** (*eis*): into, indicating transition
3. "learned" — **παιδεύω** (*paideuo*): instructed; educated; trained; he reached his full potential as an Egyptian man
4. "all" — **πάσῃ** (*pase*): all, an all-inclusive term
5. "wisdom" — **σοφία** (*sophia*): insight, skill, intelligence, philosophy, sophistication; especially bright, educated, astute, smart, or eminently enlightened.
6. "mighty" — **δυνατός** (*dunatos*): a powerful force; amazing ability; to be able, capable, or competent for any task; a force that causes one to be able or capable; one who is competent; often refers to people who have political power or political might; the idea of one who is mighty in the world's view
7. "words" — **λόγος** (*logos*): verbal communication; a masterful speaker and communicator
8. "deeds" — **ἔργον** (*ergon*): action, deed, or activity; pictures all his actions
9. "came" — **ἀναβαίνω** (*anabaino*): to rise up, to come up

SYNOPSIS

As we have seen in our first two lessons, the New Hermitage Museum located in Saint Petersburg, Russia, is a sprawling complex filled with many magnificent treasures. The extravagance of this amazing edifice is immediately noticeable upon one's arrival. Ten stunning statues of the god Atlas, each weighing ten tons and carved out of Russian black granite, line the entryway and uphold the porch that guests walk through.

Once inside, visitors begin to make their way through a series of massive rooms, such as the Dionysus Room and the Jupiter Room, which is dedicated to the display of Greek and Roman statues. One particular room, which is situated in the basement level of the Winter Palace section of the Hermitage, is called the Egyptian Room. Upon entering, one is surrounded by genuine relics from ancient Egypt. It's as if you step inside one of the ancient pyramids of Cairo as you are met with caskets, coffins, and even a mummy that dates back to the seventh century BC.

The pyramids, the sphinx, and the treasure cities of pharaoh are very real — just as real is the documented existence of a man named Moses who was born during the reign of Thutmose I and raised by his daughter. The first few chapters of Exodus, along with selected passages in the books of Acts and Hebrews, shed an interesting light on the life of this powerful patriarch.

The emphasis of this lesson:

After Moses had been educated and fully trained up in the ways of the Egyptians, the call of God on his life began to wake up inside of him. New feelings and new thinking came alive in his mind, and he began the process of discovering his God-ordained purpose as the deliverer of the nation of Israel.

A REVIEW OF LESSON 2

Moses Was Hidden for Three Months

In our last lesson, we learned about the uniqueness of Moses' parents. According to Exodus 6:20, Moses' father was named Amram, and his mother was Jochebed. The Bible says, "And there went a man [Amram] of the house of Levi, and took to wife [Jochebed] a daughter of Levi. And the woman conceived, and bare a son: and when she saw him that he was a goodly child, she hid him three months" (Exodus 2:1,2).

Acts 7:20 and Hebrews 11:23 confirm that Moses was indeed hidden for three months. They could see from the beginning that there was something unusual and special about Moses. He was polished, elegant, and sophisticated. Even though Pharaoh had commanded that every Hebrew male child born was to be killed, Moses' parents were not afraid of his edict. They had a word from God about their newborn son and they did everything they knew to do to protect and preserve his purpose.

He Was Then Placed in an 'Ark of Deliverance'

The Bible says, "And when she [Jochebed] could not longer hide him, she took for him an ark of bulrushes, and daubed it with slime and with pitch, and put the child therein; and she laid it in the flags by the river's brink" (Exodus 2:3). We saw that the word "ark" in this verse is the same word used for the "ark" that Noah constructed hundreds of years earlier. More than likely, the story of the ark that delivered Noah and his family from the catastrophic flood had strongly influenced Jochebed and Amram. So much so that she fashioned a tiny ark of bulrushes for Moses, believing it to be an "ark of deliverance" for her son and carry him to safety.

Exodus 2:4-6 goes on to say, "And his sister stood afar off, to wit what would be done to him. And the daughter of Pharaoh came down to wash herself at the river; and her maidens walked along by the river's side; and when she saw the ark among the flags, she sent her maid to fetch it. And when she had opened it, she saw the child: and, behold, the babe wept. And she had compassion on him, and said, This is one of the Hebrews' children."

Amazingly, God supernaturally guided the tiny ark through the currents of the Nile River, bringing it into the hands of the pharaoh's daughter. There, Moses would be provided for and completely prepared for his divine purpose.

Moses' Biological Mother Laid a Godly Foundation in His Life

Meanwhile, watching from the sidelines of the water's edge was Moses' sister Miriam. Once the tiny ark made it into the hands of the pharaoh's daughter, the Bible says, "Then said his sister to Pharaoh's daughter, Shall I go and call to thee a nurse of the Hebrew women, that she may nurse the child for thee? And Pharaoh's daughter said to her, Go. And the maid went and called the child's mother. And Pharaoh's daughter said unto her, Take this child away, and nurse it for me, and I will give thee thy wages. And the woman took the child, and nursed it" (Exodus 2:7-9).

After releasing and entrusting the precious gift of her son into God's hands, God brought Moses back to his mother to teach and train him in his most formative years. And she was paid to do it! Only God could orchestrate such a plan as to enable Jochebed, Moses' mother, to rear her own son in the midst of Pharaoh's murderous command. This tells us Moses' most impressionable years were spent with his mother who instilled the truth about God into him at that early age.

Proverbs 22:6 tells us, "Train up a child in the way he should go: and when he is old, he will not depart from it." Although it appeared that Moses had departed from what Jochebed had taught him during his years in the palace of Egypt, the truth had not left him. Later on, at just the right time, his mother's godly words of instruction awakened the call of God on his life and began to propel Moses toward his divine purpose.

The Name 'Moses' Is Derived From 'Thutmose'

Time passed, and Exodus 2:10 says, "And the child grew, and she [Jochebed] brought him unto Pharaoh's daughter, and he became her son. And she (Pharaoh's daughter) called his name Moses: and she said, Because I drew him out of the water."

We learned that the name "Moses" is an Egyptian name, and it is derived from the name "Thutmose," which was the family name of the current ruling pharaoh — the family Moses grew up in. History tells us that there were many Egyptian pharaohs whose name was Thutmose, meaning "born of Thoth," including Thutmose I, Thutmose II, and Thutmose III.

Thoth was the Egyptian god of writing, magic, wisdom, sophistication, and development. It was believed that he was self-created, self-existing, and self-sufficient. This helps us grasp the significance of why God introduced Himself to Moses at Mount Sinai as I AM THAT I AM. It was God's way of correcting Moses' thinking and letting him know that only God is the real self-existing, All-Sufficient One.

Moses Was Highly Educated in All the Wisdom of Egypt

Once Moses was brought back into the daughter of pharaoh's home, the Bible says, "...Pharaoh's daughter took him up, and nourished him for her own son" (Acts 7:21). The word "nourished" here is the Greek word *anatrepho*, which means *to rear*; *to nourish*; *to educate*; or *to train*. And the word "for" is the Greek word *eis*, which means *into* and indicates *transition* or the idea of *movement*. The use of this word *eis* tells us that Pharaoh's daughter was moving Moses into position to become her own son and eventually inherit the throne of Egypt.

The Bible goes on to say, "And Moses was learned in all the wisdom of the Egyptians, and was mighty in words and in deeds" (Acts 7:22). The word "learned" in this verse is a form of the Greek word *paideuo*, which means to be *instructed*, *educated*, or *trained*. It conveys the idea that Moses had reached his *full potential* as an Egyptian man.

Specifically, the Scripture says Moses was educated and trained "...in all the wisdom of the Egyptians" (Acts 7:22). The word "all" in Greek is the term *pase*, which means *all* and is an *all-inclusive* term. And the word "wisdom" is the Greek word *sophia*, and it describes *insight*, *skill*, *intelligence*, *philosophy*, and *sophistication*. It depicts *one who is especially bright, educated, astute, smart, or eminently enlightened*. This is how the Bible describes Moses as an Egyptian man.

Think of it. He was raised to know all the cutting-edge science and mathematics and schooled in the most up-to-date literature, grammar, philosophy, geography, history, and music. Moses was even trained in the religious beliefs of the Egyptians, which would come into play in unique and powerful ways once he fully entered his calling as Israel's deliverer.

He Was 'Mighty' in 'Words and Deeds'

In addition to being highly educated, the Bible says Moses was "...mighty in words and in deeds" (Acts 7:22). The word "mighty" is a translation of the Greek word *dunatos*, and it describes *a powerful force* or *amazing ability*. It means *to be able, capable, or competent for any task*. It depicts *a force that causes one to be able or capable*; *one who is competent*. This word *dunatos* — translated here as "mighty" — often refers to people who have political power or political might. Thus in the world's view, Moses was *a powerful force with amazing ability — able, capable, and competent for any task*.

This passage specifically says Moses was mighty in "words and in deeds." The term "words" here is a form of the Greek word *logos*, which describes *verbal communication* or *a masterful speaker and communicator*. So contrary to what you may have heard, Moses was a masterful speaker and communicator before he went into the wilderness for 40 years.

Furthermore, he was also a mighty — awesome force — in "deeds." This word "deeds" is the Greek word *ergon*, which depicts an *action, deed,* or *activity*. Here it pictures all Moses' actions. Hence, all of the words he spoke and every action he made were *mighty*. He was a force to be reckoned with.

The Egyptians Viewed Moses as a God

Turning our attention once more to Exodus 2:10 it says, "And the child grew, and she [Jochebed, Moses' mother] brought him unto Pharaoh's daughter, and he became her son. And she called his name Moses: and she said, Because I drew him out of the water." Pharaoh's daughter named the child Moses because she drew him from the water. The name "Moses" means *drawn out of water*.

Think about it. What water was he drawn out of? It was the Nile River. Remember, the Egyptians believed that the Nile River was the giver of all life to Egypt and the birthplace of the gods. The Nile was revered as the "Father of Life" and the "Mother of All Men." It was considered to be a manifestation of the god Hapi, who blessed the land with life, as well as with the goddess Ma'at, who embodied the concepts of truth, harmony, and balance. The Nile was also linked to the god Khnum who was the god of rebirth and creation and was originally the god of the Nile who controlled its flow and sent yearly floods which the people depended on to fertilize the land.

So when Pharaoh's daughter called him "Moses," it was the equivalent of saying:

- Moses was a gift of the gods to the people…
- Moses was to be a source of life to the Egyptians…
- Moses was to be a life-giver to Egypt…
- Moses was to bring harmony and balance to Egypt…
- Moses was a rebirth of the deity for Egypt…

Thus, Moses was elevated to the rank of an Egyptian god.

Moses Was Handsome, Brilliant, and Powerful

Writing about the character and appearance of Moses, Josephus said:

> Now Moses's understanding became superior to his age; nay far beyond that standard: and when he was taught, he discovered greater quickness of apprehension than was usual at his age: and his actions at that time promised greater, when he should come to the age of a man. God did also give him that tallness… and as for his beauty, there was no body so unpolite, as when they saw Moses they were not greatly surprized at the beauty of his countenance. Moses therefore, when he was born, and brought up in the foregoing manner, and came to the age of maturity, made his virtue manifest to the Egyptians….[1]

Here we see that Moses was very handsome, intellectually brilliant, and greatly impressive on multiple levels. Again, this is what we find in Acts 7:22, which says, "And Moses was learned in all the wisdom of the Egyptians, and was mighty in words and in deeds."

Josephus also informs us that Moses was also mighty militarily. He said:

> …The Ethiopians, who are next neighbors to the Egyptians, made an inroad into their country, which they seized upon, and carried off the effects of the Egyptians… so Moses, at the persuasion both of Thermuthis and the King himself, cheerfully undertook the business... Those of the Egyptians, at once overcame their enemies by his valor… Moses prevented the enemies… he came upon the Ethiopians, before they expected him; and joining battle with them, he beat them, and deprived them of the hopes they had of success against the Egyptians: and went on in overthrowing their cities, and indeed made a great slaughter of the Ethiopians.[2]

Keep in mind, this is who Moses was *before* the call of God was awakened in his life. He was a mighty man among all men — a powerful force to be reckoned with. He was strikingly attractive, an amazing orator, incredibly intelligent, and capable to carry out any task he undertook. Indeed, he was positioned to eventually inherit the throne of Egypt. It's no wonder the Egyptians saw him as a gift of the gods.

At Age Forty, the 'Deliverer' Began To Awaken in Moses

Then something unexpected took place. The Bible says, "And it came to pass in those days, when Moses was grown, that he went out unto his brethren, and looked on their burdens: and he spied an Egyptian smiting an Hebrew, one of his brethren" (Exodus 2:11).

The word "grown" in this verse means grown *in age* and *in responsibility*. Pharaoh had appointed Moses to be in charge of the palace. He had led the Egyptian armies in victory against the Ethiopians and had been raised to reign over Egypt at the appointed time in his future.

Yet, deep down inside he knew that he was a Hebrew — the son of Amram and Jochebed. Although he had spent most of his childhood and early adult years in an aggressively anti-Semitic environment, his biological mother had taught him in his earliest years and had deposited the Word of God into him. In that moment, when Moses saw the extreme abuse of one of his fellow Hebrews at the hands of an Egyptian, the Proverbs 22:6 principle suddenly began to kick in. The training he had received from his mother was now waking up to the call of God on his life.

Stephen talked about the great awakening of Moses in Acts 7:23, saying, "And when he was full forty years old, it came into his heart to visit his brethren the children of Israel." The word "came" is the Greek word *anabaino*, and it means *to rise up* or *to come up*. After 40 years of life — the majority of which were spent growing up in the palace and experiencing life as an Egyptian — Moses suddenly had a desire welling up in him to visit his brethren.

The word "visit" here is the Greek word *episkeptomai*, which means *to look upon, to physically visit, to care for, to inspect,* or *to provide help for those in need*. After living a very separated life with no connection to his fellow Hebrews, he suddenly wanted to personally visit and observe how the Israelites were getting along. Exodus 2:11 says, "...He went out unto his brethren, and looked on their burdens...." That is, Moses went out to inspect their conditions — then he saw an Egyptian brutally beating a fellow Hebrew. The Bible says, "And he looked this way and that way, and when he saw that there was no man, he slew the Egyptian, and hid him in the sand" (Exodus 2:12).

When Moses saw the tyrannical injustice brought against one of his own, the deliverer inside of him was roused and began to swing into action. More than likely, he was confused by and ashamed of his rash actions, so he hid the body of the man he killed in the sand. The Bible says, "Now when Pharaoh heard this thing, he sought to slay Moses. But Moses fled from the face of Pharaoh, and dwelt in the land of Midian..." (Exodus 2:15).

Moses Delivered the Daughters of the Priest in Midian

Interestingly, as soon as Moses arrived in Midian, the deliverer inside of him rose up again. Scripture says, "Now the priest of Midian had seven daughters: and they came and drew water, and filled the troughs to water their father's flock. And the shepherds came and drove them away: but Moses stood up and helped them, and watered their flock" (Exodus 2:16,17). Even though Moses didn't know these girls, when he saw them being treated unjustly, an internal alarm went off, and he could not sit by idly and do nothing.

Exodus 2:18 and 19 goes on to say, "And when they [the seven daughters] came to Reuel their father, he said, How is it that ye are come so soon to day? And they said, An Egyptian *delivered* us out of the hand of the shepherds, and also drew water enough for us, and watered the flock." Notice what these girls said about Moses: "He delivered us." Here we see total strangers declaring God's call on Moses' life.

From that moment on, Moses was welcomed into this lively family and was given one of the daughter's hand in marriage. Many years passed as they did life together and Moses became a shepherd of his father-in-law's sheep. Meanwhile, the Bible says, "God heard their [the children of Israel's] groaning, and God remembered his covenant with Abraham, with Isaac, and with Jacob. And God looked upon the children of Israel, and God had respect unto them" (Exodus 2:24,25).

It was time for the deliverer to come forth, and that deliverer was Moses. In our next lesson, we'll see how God called to him from the burning bush and began to move forward into the full light of his plan and purpose.

STUDY QUESTIONS

Study to shew thyself approved unto God, a workman that needeth not to be ashamed, rightly dividing the word of truth.
— 2 Timothy 2:15

1. What stands out to you about Moses' life during the first 40 years (*before* he left Egypt and began living in Midian)?
2. Take a few moments to jot down what you learned about the Egyptian's beliefs concerning the Nile River. How were their views linked to the gods of Egypt, and how did these beliefs affect their perception of Moses?
3. At age 40, the deliverer began to come alive inside of Moses, and he delivered one of his fellow Hebrews who was being abused by an Egyptian taskmaster. What does Exodus 2:13 and 14 say happened the very next day when Moses went out and saw two Hebrews fighting each other? What does this say to you about *knowing* the call of God on your life and *actively fulfilling* that call?

PRACTICAL APPLICATION

But be ye doers of the word, and not hearers only, deceiving your own selves.
— James 1:22

1. Moses was uniquely wired to be Israel's deliverer. Do you know what God has uniquely wired you to be? That is, what do you understand His calling to be on your life?
2. Sometimes when the call of God on your life begins to wake up in you, you begin to have unexpected desires and feelings and act in ways you never have before. Have you ever experienced such a situation? If so, describe what took place.
3. Oftentimes your calling is something that comes naturally or instinctively — something you're gifted to do both physically and spiritually. It is even often confirmed by what other people regularly reach out to you for help with. If you don't know what the call of God is on your life, take time now to pray and ask Him to reveal it to you.

---

[1] Flavius Josephus, "The Words of Flavius Josephus: Translated by William Whiston;

Antiquities of the Jews," Book II, chap. 9.6.

[2] Flavius Josephus, "The Words of Flavius Josephus: Translated by William Whiston; Antiquities of the Jews," Book II, chap. 10.1,2.

LESSON 4

TOPIC

The Encounter on Mount Horeb

SCRIPTURES

1. **Exodus 3:1-22** — Now Moses kept the flock of Jethro his father in law, the priest of Midian: and he led the flock to the backside of the desert, and came to the mountain of God, even to Horeb. And the angel of the Lord appeared unto him in a flame of fire out of the midst of a bush: and he looked, and, behold, the bush burned with fire, and the bush was not consumed. And Moses said, I will now turn aside, and see this great sight, why the bush is not burnt. And when the Lord saw that he turned aside to see, God called unto him out of the midst of the bush, and said, Moses, Moses. And he said, Here am I. And he said, Draw not nigh hither: put off thy shoes from off thy feet, for the place whereon thou standest is holy ground. Moreover he said, I am the God of thy father, the God of Abraham, the God of Isaac, and the God of Jacob. And Moses hid his face; for he was afraid to look upon God. And the Lord said, I have surely seen the affliction of my people which are in Egypt, and have heard their cry by reason of their taskmasters; for I know their sorrows. And I am come down to deliver them out of the hand of the Egyptians, and to bring them up out of that land unto a good land and a large, unto a land flowing with milk and honey; unto the place of the Canaanites, and the Hittites, and the Amorites, and the Perizzites, and the Hivites, and the Jebusites. Now therefore, behold, the cry of the children of Israel is come unto me: and I have also seen the oppression wherewith the Egyptians oppress them. Come now therefore, and I will send thee unto Pharaoh, that thou mayest bring forth my people the children of Israel out of Egypt. And Moses said unto God, Who am I, that I should go unto Pharaoh, and that I should bring forth the children

of Israel out of Egypt? And he said, Certainly I will be with thee; and this shall be a token unto thee, that I have sent thee: When thou hast brought forth the people out of Egypt, ye shall serve God upon this mountain. And Moses said unto God, Behold, when I come unto the children of Israel, and shall say unto them, The God of your fathers hath sent me unto you; and they shall say to me, What is his name? what shall I say unto them? And God said unto Moses, I AM THAT I AM: and he said, Thus shalt thou say unto the children of Israel, I AM hath sent me unto you. And God said moreover unto Moses, Thus shalt thou say unto the children of Israel, The Lord God of your fathers, the God of Abraham, the God of Isaac, and the God of Jacob, hath sent me unto you: this is my name for ever, and this is my memorial unto all generations. Go, and gather the elders of Israel together, and say unto them, The Lord God of your fathers, the God of Abraham, of Isaac, and of Jacob, appeared unto me, saying, I have surely visited you, and seen that which is done to you in Egypt. And I have said, I will bring you up out of the affliction of Egypt unto the land of the Canaanites, and the Hittites, and the Amorites, and the Perizzites, and the Hivites, and the Jebusites, unto a land flowing with milk and honey. And they shall hearken to thy voice: and thou shalt come, thou and the elders of Israel, unto the king of Egypt, and ye shall say unto him, The Lord God of the Hebrews hath met with us: and now let us go, we beseech thee, three days' journey into the wilderness, that we may sacrifice to the Lord our God. And I am sure that the king of Egypt will not let you go, no, not by a mighty hand. And I will stretch out my hand, and smite Egypt with all my wonders which I will do in the midst thereof: and after that he will let you go. And I will give this people favour in the sight of the Egyptians: and it shall come to pass, that, when ye go, ye shall not go empty. But every woman shall borrow of her neighbour, and of her that sojourneth in her house, jewels of silver, and jewels of gold, and raiment: and ye shall put them upon your sons, and upon your daughters; and ye shall spoil the Egyptians.

2. **2 Thessalonians 1:6** — Seeing it is a righteous thing with God to recompense tribulation to them that trouble you.

GREEK WORDS

There are no Greek words in this lesson.

SYNOPSIS

As we have seen, the New Hermitage Museum in Saint Petersburg, Russia, is truly a marvelous sight to behold. In addition to the Dionysus Room and the Jupiter Room, there is another amazing place called the Twenty-Column Room. Its multi-pillar design is a depiction of an ancient Greek temple. The walls of the room are lined with cabinets that are filled with genuine Greek earthenware and vases — some that date back to the eighth century BC.

Of course, there's also the mysterious Egyptian Room located in the basement of the Winter Palace section of the Hermitage. Stepping into this room is like stepping into the pages of Scripture — specifically the book of Exodus. Immediately, you are surrounded by ancient papyrus scrolls, stone tablets with hieroglyphic etchings, and Egyptian caskets and coffins that are centuries old. This room serves as a tangible reminder that the nation of Israel really was enslaved in Egypt, and Moses really was the God-ordained deliverer that led them out of bondage.

The emphasis of this lesson:

When Moses guided the flocks to feed at Mount Horeb, he encountered God in the midst of a burning bush. God was well aware of Israel's afflictions at the hand of the Egyptians and had chosen Moses to help deliver the people from slavery. As the Great I AM, nothing and no one would stop God from setting His people free and bringing them into the Promised Land.

A BRIEF REVIEW

So far in our study, we have seen that the infant Moses was placed in a basket at three months of age and set afloat on the Nile River. After being retrieved by the Pharaoh's daughter, God divinely arranged for him to be nursed and cared for by his Hebrew birth mother during his most formidable years. It is likely that Moses went to live in Pharaoh's palace at about the age of five. This means that for about 35 years, he lived apart from the people of Israel and was thoroughly educated and trained in Egyptian ways. According to the Jewish historian Josephus, Moses became the prince of Egypt and was in training to become the next pharaoh.

Then at the age of 40, the call of God began to wake up inside of him. One day when he went out to inspect the conditions of his Hebrew kin, he witnessed one of the Israelites being brutally abused by an Egyptian. Enraged by the injustice, Moses rose up and killed the Egyptian and then hid his body in the sand. Upon hearing that Pharaoh was seeking to kill him, Moses fled for his life to the land of Midian.

In Midian, he came upon the community's well where he met the seven daughters of the local high priest named Jethro. Seeing them be harshly treated by a band of nomadic shepherds, Moses rose up and delivered the girls by driving the shepherds away and then took time to water the girls' flock. Grateful for Moses' protection and care, Jethro welcomed him into the family and offered him his daughter Zipporah's hand in marriage. Moses came under Jethro's authority and became the fulltime shepherd of his father-in-law's flock. For the next 40 years, Moses tended sheep and lived on the backside of the desert until that fateful day when he encountered God on Mount Horeb.

Moses Drove the Flocks To Feed at Mount Horeb

As we continue the story in Exodus 3, the Bible says, "Now Moses kept the flock of Jethro his father in law, the priest of Midian: and he led the flock to the backside of the desert, and came to the mountain of God, even to Horeb" (v. 1). At this point, Moses is 80 years old, and it has been 40 years since he left Egypt. His years of living in the palace are a distant memory. His life has been so humbled that he doesn't even have a flock of his own. All the sheep he is habitually caring for belong to his father-in-law.

Nevertheless, Moses was in a God-ordained school "with a flock of sheep" to learn how to lead the "flock" of God's people in the future. As he led the animals on this particular day, Moses brought them to Mount Horeb, which was not a place shepherds usually brought their sheep to graze. The local people believed that God lived atop Horeb and therefore they stayed away from it. Although the name "Horeb" is somewhat a mystery, it probably means "desert" or "desolation" and describes the surrounding terrain where the mountain is found.

Josephus wrote about the day Moses took the flocks to Mount Horeb, stating:

> But some time afterward… he drove his flocks thither to feed them. Now this is the highest of all the mountains thereabouts; and the best for pasturage; the herbage being there good: and it

> had not been before fed upon, because of the opinion men had that God dwelt there: the shepherds not daring to ascend up to it. And here it was that a wonderful prodigy happened to Moses....[1]

Exodus 3:2 goes on to say, "And the angel of the Lord appeared unto him in a flame of fire out of the midst of a bush: and he looked, and, behold, the bush burned with fire, and the bush was not consumed." The word "behold" here carries a sense of *awe, amazement,* and *wonder*. What's interesting is that the bush burned, but it was not consumed. It burned with fire, but it did not crackle or diminish, and no leaf curled nor was any branch burned. This bush that burned but was not consumed was such a magnetic sight that it drew Moses in for a closer examination.

Interestingly, this burning would become a symbol of Moses himself — a person who burned with the fire of God but was never consumed by it.

God Called Moses by Name From the Midst of a Burning Bush

The Bible continues by saying, "And Moses said, I will now turn aside, and see this great sight, why the bush is not burnt. And when the Lord saw that he turned aside to see, God called unto him out of the midst of the bush, and said, Moses, Moses. And he said, Here am I" (Exodus 3:3,4).

Moses had seen many great sights as the privileged prince of Egypt, but he had never seen anything like this burning bush that was not consumed. When he turned to see it, God called him by name. Even though Moses was an obscure shepherd on the backside of the desert, God had not forgotten him. In fact, God was waiting for this very moment when Moses would draw near to Him and be in a position that He could speak to Moses and give him his assignment. Please note: the double calling of Moses' name — *Moses, Moses* — implies importance and urgency.

God then said, "...Draw not nigh hither: put off thy shoes from off thy feet, for the place whereon thou standest is holy ground" (v. 5). Notice that God told Moses to do two things to show special honor to this place: First, He said, *"Draw not nigh hither,"* which literally means "stop coming closer." Moses was on his way for an up-close examination of the burning bush when God stopped him. Second, God commanded Moses, *"Put off thy shoes from off thy feet."* Removing his shoes showed an appropriate *humility*. In ancient cultures, one would take off his shoes when he came into someone's house. In this case, Moses had entered God's "house"—the very presence of God was there on the mountain. *Pulling off the shoes* was also an emblem of laying aside the *pollutions* of the world.

Josephus wrote about this event and said:

> ...For a fire fed upon a thorn bush; yet did the green leaves and the flowers continue untouched; and the fire did not at all consume the fruit branches; although the flame was great and fierce. Moses was affrighted at this strange sight... but he was still more astonished when the fire uttered a voice, and called to him by name, and spake words to him; by which it signified to him how bold he had been in venturing to come into a place whither no man had ever come before; because the place was divine: and advised him to remove a great way from the flame, and to be contented with what he had seen: and though he were himself a good man, and the off-spring of great men, yet that he should not pry any farther: and he foretold to him, that he should have glory and honor among men by the blessing of God upon him. He also commanded him to go away thence with confidence to Egypt, in order to his being the commander and conductor of the body of the Hebrews; and to his delivering his own people from the injuries they suffered there....[2]

Moses Would Not Look Upon God

As Moses obediently complied with God's commands, God said, "...I am the God of thy father, the God of Abraham, the God of Isaac, and the God of Jacob. And Moses hid his face; for he was afraid to look upon God" (Exodus 3:6).

God reminded Moses that His covenant with Israel was still in force. This wasn't a "new God" meeting Moses, but the same God that dealt with Abraham, Isaac, and Jacob. Some in the days of Moses might have thought that God had forgotten His covenant in the 400 plus years of Israel's time in Egypt. But that was not the case. God was at work to preserve and to multiply the nation.

It's interesting to see that Moses hid his face and was afraid to look at God. He had been raised in Egypt to be the next pharaoh, and pharaohs were considered to be "god on earth." And as a god, no one was allowed to look into their faces. This means no one was allowed to look into the face of Moses. It was because of this knowledge that Moses hid his face and would not look at God.

God Had Seen and Heard of Israel's Afflictions

Exodus 3:7 tells us, "And the Lord said, I have surely seen the affliction of my people which are in Egypt, and have heard their cry by reason of their taskmasters; for I know their sorrows." Pay close attention to what God is saying here. He said:

- *I have seen their affliction...*
- *I have heard their cries...*
- *I know their sorrows...*

If you study the Scriptures, you'll discover two specific things that God actually hears. One is the cry of sin, which we see in Genesis 18:20 and 21. In this passage, God was visiting Abraham and said He had come to see if the *cry of sin* in Sodom and Gomorrah was as grievous as what He was hearing in Heaven. The second thing the Bible says God hears is the *cry of His people*, which is what He says here in Exodus 3:7.

In verses 8-10, God said, "And I am come down to deliver them out of the hand of the Egyptians, and to bring them up out of that land unto a good land and a large, unto a land flowing with milk and honey; unto the place of the Canaanites, and the Hittites, and the Amorites, and the Perizzites, and the Hivites, and the Jebusites. Now therefore, behold, the cry of the children of Israel is come unto me: and I have also seen the oppression wherewith the Egyptians oppress them. Come now therefore, and I will send thee unto Pharaoh, that thou mayest bring forth my people the children of Israel out of Egypt" (Exodus 3:8-10).

In this passage we see that God is delivering the children of Israel and then taking them to a new land. That is the same thing He wants to do for you. He wants to deliver you from every enslaving chain of bondage and bring you into a new land — the land of His promises, which He has spoken in His Word.

Who would be God's spokesman and function as Israel's deliverer? God handpicked Moses for the job, and the pharaoh Moses was sent to confront was probably Thutmose II. Now, you may be thinking, *If God is the One who is going to deliver the children of Israel, why did He need Moses?* The answer is, God chooses to partner with humanity and includes us in His work. Sure, He could have supernaturally done everything by Himself, but He chooses to use human instruments — including ordinary people just like you — to work together with Him to accomplish every task (*see* 2 Corinthians 6:1).

God Promised To Be With Moses

In response, the Bible says, "And Moses said unto God, Who am I, that I should go unto Pharaoh, and that I should bring forth the children of Israel out of Egypt?" (Exodus 3:11). Forty years earlier, before Moses had left Egypt, he knew exactly who he was — he was a prince of Egypt and a mighty military commander. However, after 40 years of leading sheep around the desert, Moses had lost the confidence he once had.

To encourage and reassure Moses, God said, "...Certainly I will be with thee; and this shall be a token unto thee, that I have sent thee: When thou hast brought forth the people out of Egypt, ye shall serve God upon this mountain" (Exodus 3:12). Just as God promised to be with Moses, He promises to be with *you* and everyone He sends on an assignment.

Still trying to grasp all that God was saying, Moses asked, "...Behold, when I come unto the children of Israel, and shall say unto them, The God of your fathers hath sent me unto you; and they shall say to me, What is his name? what shall I say unto them? And God said unto Moses, I AM THAT I AM: and he said, Thus shalt thou say unto the children of Israel, I AM hath sent me unto you" (Exodus 3:13,14).

The Meaning of the Name 'I AM THAT I AM'

The phrase "I AM THAT I AM" reveals *that God has no equal*, which was quite a statement seeing as the land of Egypt was filled with many gods. This name, "I AM THAT I AM," is connected with the name *Yahweh*, which was not a new name, nor an unknown name. The name *Yahweh* appears more than 160 times in the book of Genesis. God told Moses His name was I AM because God simply is, and there was never a time when He did not exist, or a time when He will cease to exist.

Moreover, the name I AM has within it the idea that God is *completely independent* — that He relies on nothing for life or existence. It is also connected with the idea that God is *eternal* and *unchanging*. Inherent in the name I AM is the sense that God is "the becoming one," which means God becomes whatever is lacking in our time of need. The name I AM invites us to fill in the blank to meet our need.

In contrast, Moses' family name was connected to Thoth — the Egyptian god who they believed to be self-created, self-existing, and self-sustaining. When Moses encountered God on Mount Horeb and God identified Himself as I AM THAT I AM, he was meeting the real deal. It was the equivalent of God saying, "Forget that god you grew up under. If you want to know the real self-existing, self-sustaining One, it's Me!" Thus, the name God gave was both an announcement and a declaration.

God Promised To Bring Israel Into Canaan

God continued to speak to Moses saying, "...Thus shalt thou say unto the children of Israel, The Lord God of your fathers, the God of Abraham, the God of Isaac, and the God of Jacob, hath sent me unto you: this is my name for ever, and this is my memorial unto all generations. Go, and gather the elders of Israel together, and say unto them, The Lord God of your fathers, the God of Abraham, of Isaac, and of Jacob, appeared unto me, saying, I have surely visited you, and seen that which is done to you in Egypt. And I have said, I will bring you up out of the affliction of Egypt unto the land of the Canaanites, and the Hittites, and the Amorites, and the Perizzites, and the Hivites, and the Jebusites, unto a land flowing with milk and honey" (Exodus 3:15-17).

Keep in mind, the children of Israel had been living in Egypt more than 400 years. God was sending Moses to announce it was time for them to go back to Canaan. The truth is, after more than four centuries of living in Egypt, they had set down roots and become settled in the land. They had even previously enjoyed a good life in Goshen. Leaving could be difficult even though they knew Canaan was their land.

The Lord then told Moses, "And they shall hearken to thy voice: and thou shalt come, thou and the elders of Israel, unto the king of Egypt, and ye shall say unto him, The Lord God of the Hebrews hath met with us: and now let us go, we beseech thee, three days' journey into the wilderness, that we may sacrifice to the Lord our God" (Exodus 3:18).

Israel's Deliverance Would Require God's Mighty Hand

Now when we come to Exodus 3:19, God makes this very powerful statement: "And I am sure that the king of Egypt will not let you go, no, not by a mighty hand." Interestingly, in the original Hebrew, this verse reads, "And I am sure that the king of Egypt will not let you go ***except*** by a mighty hand." What exactly is God saying here?

Keep in mind that God is all-knowing, and He knew what it would take to move Pharaoh. The plagues were divinely engineered for a specific purpose and were not haphazard events. How would Pharaoh ever agree to let this free-labor force leave the country? Before Moses could even ask this question, God answered it.

Since Pharaoh would not easily let go of the Israelites, God would bring plagues against Egypt to convince Pharaoh to let them go. This is what God speaks of in Exodus 3:20: "And I will stretch out my hand, and smite Egypt with all my wonders which I will do in the midst thereof: and after that he will let you go." This was God's promise to let Egypt know what it felt like to be beaten! Remember, for many decades — possibly for several hundred years — the children of Israel had been beaten into submission with rods. God was promising to "beat" Egypt as Egypt had beaten Israel.

In our next lesson, we will carefully unpack Exodus chapter 4 and look at God's promise to punish Egypt.

STUDY QUESTIONS

Study to shew thyself approved unto God, a workman that needeth not to be ashamed, rightly dividing the word of truth.
— 2 Timothy 2:15

1. One of the ways we remove contaminants from our life is through the practice of *repentance*. Carefully meditate on First John 1:9, and in your own words describe what it means to *repent* and how God responds to you when you do. (Also *consider* Acts 3:19; Psalm 32:1-6; Proverbs 28:13; Hosea 14:2.)
2. In addition to hearing the cry of sin, God also hears the cries of His people. Take time to reflect on Psalm 34:15-20 and 145:18-21. What promises does God make to you in these passages? How do they

encourage you to seek God and pour out your heart to Him? (*Consider* Psalm 62:5-8.)

PRACTICAL APPLICATION

But be ye doers of the word, and not hearers only,
deceiving your own selves.
—James 1:22

1. For Moses, pulling off his shoes in God's presence represented the removal of the *contaminants* and *pollutants* of the world. How do you prepare yourself when you come into God's presence? Is there anything you've come into contact with that is polluting your life that you need to remove from yourself? If so, what is it?
2. Reread the section on the meaning of the name "I AM THAT I AM." What aspects of this powerful and diverse title for God personally touch your heart most deeply?
3. One of the meanings of the name "I AM" is *the Becoming One*, which means God becomes whatever you need Him to be. Stop and think: *What do I need God to be for me right now?*

---

[1] Flavius Josephus, "The Words of Flavius Josephus: Translated by William Whiston; Antiquities of the Jews," Book II, chap. 12.1.

[2] Flavius Josephus, "The Words of Flavius Josephus: Translated by William Whiston; Antiquities of the Jews," Book II, chap. 12.1.

LESSON 5

TOPIC

The Promise of God To Punish Egypt

SCRIPTURES

1. **Exodus 4:1-21** — And Moses answered and said, But, behold, they will not believe me, nor hearken unto my voice: for they will say, The Lord hath not appeared unto thee. And the Lord said unto him, What is that in thine hand? And he said, A rod. And he said, Cast it

on the ground. And he cast it on the ground, and it became a serpent; and Moses fled from before it. And the Lord said unto Moses, Put forth thine hand, and take it by the tail. And he put forth his hand, and caught it, and it became a rod in his hand. That they may believe that the Lord God of their fathers, the God of Abraham, the God of Isaac, and the God of Jacob, hath appeared unto thee. And the Lord said furthermore unto him, Put now thine hand into thy bosom. And he put his hand into his bosom: and when he took it out, behold, his hand was leprous as snow. And he said, Put thine hand into thy bosom again. And he put his hand into his bosom again; and plucked it out of his bosom, and, behold, it was turned again as his other flesh. And it shall come to pass, if they will not believe thee, neither hearken to the voice of the first sign, that they will believe the voice of the latter sign. And it shall come to pass, if they will not believe also these two signs, neither hearken unto thy voice, that thou shalt take of the water of the river, and pour it upon the dry land: and the water which thou takest out of the river shall become blood upon the dry land. And Moses said unto the Lord, O my Lord, I am not eloquent, neither heretofore, nor since thou hast spoken unto thy servant: but I am slow of speech, and of a slow tongue. And the Lord said unto him, Who hath made man's mouth? or who maketh the dumb, or deaf, or the seeing, or the blind? have not I the Lord? Now therefore go, and I will be with thy mouth, and teach thee what thou shalt say. And he said, O my Lord, send, I pray thee, by the hand of him whom thou wilt send. And the anger of the Lord was kindled against Moses, and he said, Is not Aaron the Levite thy brother? I know that he can speak well… And thou shalt speak unto him, and put words in his mouth: and I will be with thy mouth, and with his mouth, and will teach you what ye shall do. And he shall be thy spokesman unto the people: and he shall be, even he shall be to thee instead of a mouth, and thou shalt be to him instead of God. And thou shalt take this rod in thine hand, wherewith thou shalt do signs. And Moses went and returned to Jethro his father in law, and said unto him, Let me go, I pray thee, and return unto my brethren which are in Egypt, and see whether they be yet alive. And Jethro said to Moses, Go in peace. And the Lord said unto Moses in Midian, Go, return into Egypt: for all the men are dead which sought thy life. And Moses took his wife and his sons, and set them upon an ass, and he returned to the land of Egypt: and Moses took the rod of God in his hand. And the Lord said unto

Moses, When thou goest to return into Egypt, see that thou do all those wonders before Pharaoh, which I have put in thine hand…

2. **Acts 7:22** — And Moses was learned in all the wisdom of the Egyptians, and was mighty in words and in deeds.

GREEK WORDS

There are no Greek words in this lesson.

SYNOPSIS

One of the most amazing things about taking a trip to Egypt today is the ability to see some of the same sites and cities people saw during the Old Testament era. One such place is called the Temple of Luxor, which is located on the Nile just across from the Valley of the Kings where many members of nobility were buried. As one approaches this temple, one would see a long row of sphinxes that line the roadway. Ruins of the Luxor complex include multiple halls and chambers and clusters of decorative columns. Luxor is believed to be the largest temple complex ever constructed, and it is one of the places still standing today that Moses himself saw when God used him to deliver the children of Israel from Egyptian bondage.

The emphasis of this lesson:

Just as Egypt had beaten the children of Israel for years on end, God promised to stretch out His hand and punish Egypt for everything they had done to His people. God used the rod in Moses' hand to work His wonders and gave Moses supernatural signs to confirm that He would indeed carry out the judgments He had spoken.

A REVIEW OF LESSON 4

Moses Encountered God on Mount Horeb

In our last lesson, we saw how God appeared to Moses at Mount Horeb and spoke to him out of a bush that burned but was not consumed. Concerning Israel, God said, "…I will bring you up out of the affliction of Egypt unto the land of the Canaanites, and the Hittites, and the Amorites, and the Perizzites, and the Hivites, and the Jebusites, unto a land flowing with milk and honey. And they [Israel] shall hearken to thy voice: and thou shalt come, thou and the elders of Israel, unto the king of Egypt, and ye shall say unto him, The Lord God of the Hebrews hath met with us: and now let us go, we beseech thee, three days' journey into the wilderness, that we may sacrifice to the Lord our God" (Exodus 3:17,18).

It Would Require God's Mighty Hand To Deliver Israel

In the very next verse, God added, "And I am sure that the king of Egypt will not let you go, no, not by a mighty hand" (Exodus 3:19). We learned that according to the original Hebrew, this verse would better be translated, "And I [God] am sure that the king of Egypt will not let you go *except* by a mighty hand." The truth is, we serve a God that is omniscient, or all-knowing, and therefore, He knew from the beginning it would take a mighty hand to get Pharaoh to release the people. There was no way Pharaoh would ever agree to allow this free-labor force to leave the country. This is why God engineered the ten plagues. They were for a specific purpose and were in no way haphazard events.

Since Pharaoh would not easily let go of the Israelites, God would bring plagues against Egypt to convince Pharaoh to let them go. This is what God refers to in Exodus 3:20: "And I will stretch out my hand, and smite Egypt with all my wonders which I will do in the midst thereof: and after that he will let you go." Notice the phrase "I will stretch out My hand and smite Egypt." This declaration is repeated numerous times throughout the Exodus account, and it was God's promise to let Egypt know what it felt like to be beaten!

As Egypt Beat Israel With Rods, God Would Beat Egypt With His Rod

Remember, for many decades — possibly for several hundred years — the Egyptians had repeatedly beaten and afflicted the children of Israel with rods. The Scripture says taskmasters had brutally forced the Israelites into slavery and made them build Pharaoh's treasure cities as well as monuments, palaces, and temples all over Egypt. In Exodus 3:20, God was promising to "beat" Egypt as Egypt had beaten Israel.

God said, "...Vengeance is mine; I will repay, saith the Lord" (Romans 12:19). We find this payback principle elaborated on even more by the apostle Paul in Second Thessalonians 1:6, which says, "Seeing it is a righteous thing with God to recompense tribulation to them that trouble you." Isn't that interesting? It is a *righteous* thing — an honorable and morally good thing — for God to bring a just recompense of trouble on those who trouble you, His child.

Taking into account the original Greek meaning in this verse, here is the *Renner Interpretive Version* (*RIV*) of Second Thessalonians 1:6:

> **God is always just and fair, so you can be sure that He will repay those people who put you through all this misery. He will reimburse those who have afflicted you and see to it that they receive a full settlement of double trouble for the traumatic circumstances they put you through. God has a habit of being fair, so you can be certain that He will make sure everyone gets exactly what is deserved.**

Because Pharaoh and the Egyptian people beat Israel with rods, now God Himself was going to strike Egypt with His rod of correction.

Israel Was Paid in Full As They Left Egypt

The third chapter of Exodus concludes with God saying, "And I will give this people [the children of Israel] favour in the sight of the Egyptians: and it shall come to pass, that, when ye go, ye shall not go empty. But every woman shall borrow of her neighbour, and of her that sojourneth in her house, jewels of silver, and jewels of gold, and raiment: and ye shall put them upon your sons, and upon your daughters; and ye shall spoil the Egyptians" (Exodus 3:21,22).

This is a fulfillment of Deuteronomy 15:12-15 in which God instructed the Israelites that if they had a Hebrew man or woman who had sold themselves in service as a slave, after six years their service was finished. When they set their fellow Hebrew free at the beginning of the seventh year, they were not to let them go away empty handed.

When the nation of Israel left Egypt, God Himself made sure that they were paid in full for all their past labors. They had exerted years of intense toil but had never been paid for what they had done. All that changed on the day of the Exodus. God saw to it that His people were abundantly blessed as they left the land of Egypt.

Moses' First Objection: 'They Won't Believe Me or Listen to Me'

When we come to Exodus 4, we find Moses beginning to offer God objections as to why he is not the right person to deliver Israel. He begins by saying, "But, behold, they will not believe me, nor hearken unto my voice: for they will say, The Lord hath not appeared unto thee" (Exodus 4:1). Actually, Jewish historian Josephus commented specifically on this, saying:

> But Moses was astonished at what he saw, and much more at what he heard... But said, 'I am still in doubt how I, who am a private man, and one of no abilities, should either persuade my own countrymen to leave the country they now inhabit, and to follow me to a land whither I lead them: or, if they should be persuaded, how can I force Pharaoh to permit them to depart; since they augment their own wealth and prosperity by the labors and works they put upon them.'[1]

Now this was a very logical observation and question Moses offered. In the eyes of the Egyptians, the pharaoh was more than a man. He was viewed as a god in all Egypt. The entire nation revered him and lived to serve his every wish. Indeed, the pharaoh's power and authority was supreme, and there was no constitution, law, or legislature even remotely equal to him. The pharaohs were said to be the children of the sun and the friends of the greatest gods of Egypt. They sat with the gods in their own temples and were worshiped right alongside them.

Having grown up in the royal courts of Egypt, Moses knew all these things. But he also knew what happened behind the scenes and that Pharaoh was just a mortal man like any other man. Having been commissioned by the authority of the living God, Moses was to confront Pharaoh and demand he let the Israelites go.

God Answered Moses: 'Use What's in Your Hand'

In Exodus 4:2, God responded to Moses and said, "...What is that in thine hand? And he said, A rod." What's interesting is that this rod in Moses' hand would later be called *the rod of God* in Exodus 4:20 and 17:9. God used what Moses had in his hand — a simple shepherd's staff — to carry out His will. And in the same way, God will use whatever you have in your hand to accomplish the assignment He has given you!

Examples of this in Scripture include:

- God used the ox goad that was in Shamgar's hand (Judges 3:31).
- God used the sling and the stone in David's hand (1 Samuel 17:49).
- God used the jawbone of a donkey in Samson's hand (Judges 15:15).
- God used five loaves and two fish in the hand of a little boy (John 6:9).

Once Moses stepped out in obedience, God drew attention to the "rod" that was in his hand. It was with that rod that the Red Sea would part. That rod would strike a rock and water would pour forth. That rod would also be raised when Israel was in battle, and as long as it was lifted, the children of Israel would be victorious.

After Moses told God that a rod was in his hand, God said, "Cast it on the ground. And he cast it on the ground, and it became a serpent; and Moses fled from before it" (Exodus 4:3).

Josephus commented on this incident, saying:

> God persuaded him to be courageous on all occasions and promised to be with him, and to assist him in his words when he was to persuade men; and in his deeds when he was to perform wonders. He bid him also to take a signal of the truth of what he said, by throwing his rod upon the ground: which when he had done, it crept along, and was become a serpent, and rolled itself round in its folds, and erected its head, as ready to revenge itself on such as should assault it. After which it become a rod again as it was before.[2]

The Significance of the Rod Becoming a Serpent

Have you ever wondered why God turned Moses' rod into a snake? The answer to this question is very important. In ancient Egypt, the serpent — specifically the cobra with its hooded head — is found in Egyptian art. It's also carved into furniture, found on pillars and columns, and depicted on vessels that were used by royalty and the upper classes. The cobra was worn as jewelry — often on arm bands and around people's fingers — and it was always on the front circlet of the crown for Pharaoh. Cobra heads were even popular amulets in ancient Egypt.

A cobra often represented the god Hathor or Sekhmet who were Egyptian messengers and avengers of the sun god Ra. Egyptians believed that Ra gave the cobra as an emblem of might and protection — and that this sign provided special protection for Pharaoh's descendants (the next pharaohs).

For ancient Egyptians, the cobra was a Pharaonic symbol of power and protection. The image of the rearing, hooded cobra both protected the king and projected his power. It was believed that the gods defended him who wore a cobra crown. Cobras were also represented as guardians of temples and sacred sanctuaries.

When Moses' threw his rod down, it became a *real snake* — a cobra that was so real it frightened Moses and caused him to run from it. In that moment, "...The Lord said unto Moses, Put forth thine hand, and take it by the tail. And he put forth his hand, and caught it, and it became a rod in his hand. That they may believe that the Lord God of their fathers, the God of Abraham, the God of Isaac, and the God of Jacob, hath appeared unto thee" (Exodus 4:4,5).

Notice God told Moses to "take it by the tail." That is the most dangerous way to handle a snake. Nevertheless, Moses obeyed God's instructions, and by faith he reached out and grabbed the snake by the tail and was unharmed. Moses learned to do what God told him to do, even when it was not comfortable. Moses' rod would become a symbol of power and protection for him and the nation of Israel.

The Power Displayed Through the Sign of Leprosy

To give Moses even more credibility in the eyes of his fellow Hebrews, God gave him a second sign to prove he had been sent by God. The Bible says, "And the Lord said furthermore unto him, Put now thine hand into thy bosom. And he put his hand into his bosom: and when he took it out, behold, his hand was leprous as snow. And he said, Put thine hand into thy bosom again. And he put his hand into his bosom again; and plucked it out of his bosom, and, behold, it was turned again as his other flesh" (Exodus 4:6,7).

To truly understand the weight of this wondrous sign, we have to realize that leprosy was a terrifying disease in the ancient world. Today, it would be like the equivalent of someone contracting an aggressive form of cancer or HIV. Leprosy was terrifying because people believed there was no cure for it and it spread rapidly. So when God made Moses' hand leprous and then instantly cured him of the leprosy, it was truly a display of supernatural power in their eyes. God told Moses, "And it shall come to pass, if they will not believe thee, neither hearken to the voice of the first sign, that they will believe the voice of the latter sign" (Exodus 4:8).

The Meaning Behind the Water Turning to Blood

The Lord then added, "And it shall come to pass, if they will not believe also these two signs, neither hearken unto thy voice, that thou shalt take of the water of the river, and pour it upon the dry land: and the water which thou takest out of the river shall become blood upon the dry land" (Exodus 4:9).

Remember what we learned in our previous lessons: The Nile River was viewed as a god — and the birthplace of all the gods and life. By turning its water into blood — which was repulsive to Egyptians — God was declaring judgment on all the gods of Egypt.

Josephus weighed in on the importance of all three signs given by God saying:

> He also, upon God's command took some of the water that was near him, and poured it upon the ground, and saw the color was that of blood. Upon the wonder that Moses shewed at these signs, God exhorted him to be of good courage; and to be assured that he would be the greatest support to him; and bid him make use of those signs in order to obtain belief among all men, that thou art sent by me; and dost all things according to my commands. Accordingly I enjoin thee to make no more delays but to make haste to Egypt, and to travel night and day, and not to draw out the time, and so make the slavery of the Hebrews, and their sufferings to last the longer.[3]

Moses' Second Objection: 'I Am Slow of Speech'

You might think that after God gave Moses all these visible manifestations of His remarkable power he would be supercharged with faith and convinced of success in his divine assignment. But that was not the case. Once more, Moses voiced his doubts and fears to the Lord saying,

"...O my Lord, I am not eloquent, neither heretofore, nor since thou hast spoken unto thy servant: but I am slow of speech, and of a slow tongue" (Exodus 4:10).

These words reveal that Moses was not confident with his ability to speak. The phrase "slow of speech" literally means "heavy of mouth." The irony here is that 40 years earlier, Moses was not slow of speech or slow of tongue at all. According to Acts 7:22, "...Moses was learned in all the wisdom of the Egyptians, and was *mighty in words* and in deeds." When he was living in the palace as a prince of Egypt, he was a masterful communicator of the Egyptian language. However, after tending sheep for four decades and not speaking Egyptian, he had become quite rusty in his speech and had lost his keen eloquence.

When Moses said, "...O my Lord, I am not eloquent...I am slow of speech, and of a slow tongue (Exodus 4:10)," he was saying, "Lord, please don't send me. I'm only a shadow of what I used to be." Clearly it would be humiliating for Moses to return to Egypt. His pride was balking — flinching and pulling back — against the will of God. His self-confidence and self-reliance on his flesh were gone. As strange as it may seem, this place of humility is usually the place we are most ready to be used by God.

God Answered Moses: 'I Will Teach You What To Say'

Moments after those fearful words left Moses' lips, the Bible says, "And the Lord said unto him, Who hath made man's mouth? or who maketh the dumb, or deaf, or the seeing, or the blind? have not I the Lord? Now therefore go, and I will be with thy mouth, and teach thee what thou shalt say" (Exodus 4:11,12).

To bring peace to Moses' heart and mind and eliminate feelings of inadequacy, God promised to be with Moses' mouth and teach him what to say. **The greatest truth that annihilates fear is God's promise to always be with us.** Again and again throughout Scripture, He tells us He will never leave us or forsake us. And like He promised Moses, He has also promised us to give us the words we need to speak the moment we need them (*see* Luke 12:11,12).

Once more Moses objected. "And he said, O my Lord, send, I pray thee, by the hand of him whom thou wilt send" (Exodus 4:13). In other words,

"Send somebody else, God. Don't send me." Moses was so focused on his inabilities he just couldn't seem to break free.

It's important to note that God wasn't upset when Moses said, "Who am I, Lord?" (*See* Exodus 3:11.) Nor was He irritated when Moses asked, "Who shall I say has sent me? (*See* Exodus 3:13.) Likewise, God wasn't annoyed when Moses asked, "But what if they don't believe me or listen to my voice?" (*See* Exodus 4:1.) Neither was God angered when Moses declared, "I am not eloquent..." (*See* Exodus 4:10).

However, when Moses continued to reject God's assignment and ask for another person to be sent in his place, the Bible says, "And the anger of the Lord was kindled against Moses, and he said, Is not Aaron the Levite thy brother? I know that he can speak well..." (*see* Exodus 4:14).

Aaron's Role in Moses' Life

Remember, Aaron had been in Egypt all along, and for the 40 years Moses had been in Midian, Aaron had been speaking Egyptian fluently. However, Aaron was not God's pick to be His mouthpiece. The Scripture reveals that eventually Aaron turned out to be a source of many problems for Moses.

- Aaron instigated the worship of the golden calf (Exodus 32:1-6).
- Aaron's sons blasphemed God with impure offerings (Leviticus 10:1-7).
- Aaron even led a mutiny against Moses (Numbers 12:1-8).

In spite of the trouble God knew Aaron would bring about, He allowed Moses to team up with Aaron in leadership. God said, "And thou shalt speak unto him, and put words in his mouth: and I will be with thy mouth, and with his mouth, and will teach you what ye shall do. And he shall be thy spokesman unto the people: and he shall be, even he shall be to thee instead of a mouth, and thou shalt be to him instead of God" (Exodus 4:15,16).

This passage tells us that Aaron became Moses' *prophet.* He became like an *interpreter* for Moses. God knew that Aaron could speak well, and therefore Aaron would do all the speaking to Pharaoh for Moses. Yet although Aaron was a smooth talker, he was a man weak on content. To be clear: Aaron wasn't God's spokesman. He was the spokesman of Moses.

God concluded His instruction to Moses saying, "And thou shalt take this rod in thine hand, wherewith thou shalt do signs" (Exodus 4:17). Although God allowed Aaron to speak for Moses, He told Moses to hold tightly to and carry the rod. The rod represented God's power and authority.

In our next lesson, we will continue our walk through Exodus and see what happened when God sent Moses to Pharaoh to demand that the Israelites be set free.

STUDY QUESTIONS

Study to shew thyself approved unto God, a workman that needeth not to be ashamed, rightly dividing the word of truth.
— 2 Timothy 2:15

1. When God called Moses to be His mouthpiece before Pharaoh and deliver the children of Israel, what excuses did Moses offer (*see* Exodus 3:11; 4:1,10)? Can you identify with any of these objections?
2. The Egyptians believed that the serpent — specifically the cobra — symbolized power and protection. When Moses had Aaron throw down his rod, what did his rod (his serpent) do to the rods (serpents) of the Egyptian magicians (*see* Exodus 7:10-12). What do you think God was saying to Pharaoh and the Egyptians through this demonstration of His divine power?
3. The greatest truth that annihilates fear is God's promise to always be with you. This is a guarantee He speaks again and again throughout Scripture. Take time to look up and write down these verses that assure you of God's *permanent presence* in your life.
   - Joshua 1:9
   - Isaiah 41:10 and 43:2
   - Hebrews 13:5,6
   - 1 John 2:27

PRACTICAL APPLICATION

But be ye doers of the word, and not hearers only, deceiving your own selves.
— James 1:22

1. After 40 years of being out of the loop of Egyptian life, Moses felt very inadequate to be God's spokesman before Pharaoh. If you're feeling inadequate to do what God has asked you to do, spend a few minutes meditating on the truth of Second Corinthians 12:9,10 (in a few different versions). What is the Holy Spirit speaking to you personally in this passage?
2. When Moses continued to argue with God about his inability to carry out God's assignment, God allowed Moses to team up with Aaron. But Aaron ended up causing Moses and the Israelites many problems. Is there someone you're teamed up with that is not necessarily God's choice — someone that's actually causing you problems as you're trying to fulfill God's assignment? Pray and ask the Holy Spirit to show you anyone you need to disconnect from and to give you the grace to trust Him as you walk out your calling.
3. What has God asked *you* to do for Him? Have you done it? Or have you given Him excuses or reasons why you can't do it? If so, what are they? Pray and ask God to speak His words of encouragement and reassurance to do what He's asked you to do. Write what He tells you.

---

[1] Flavius Josephus, "The Words of Flavius Josephus: Translated by William Whiston; Antiquities of the Jews," Book II, chap. 12.2.

[2] Flavius Josephus, "The Words of Flavius Josephus: Translated by William Whiston; Antiquities of the Jews," Book II, chap. 12.3.

[3] Flavius Josephus, "The Words of Flavius Josephus: Translated by William Whiston; Antiquities of the Jews," Book II, chap. 12.3.

LESSON 6

TOPIC

God Sends Moses to Pharaoh

SCRIPTURES

1. **Exodus 4:27-31** — And the Lord said to Aaron, Go into the wilderness to meet Moses. And he went, and met him in the mount of God, and kissed him. And Moses told Aaron all the words of the

LORD who had sent him, and all the signs which he had commanded him. And Moses and Aaron went and gathered together all the elders of the children of Israel: And Aaron spake all the words which the LORD had spoken unto Moses, and did the signs in the sight of the people. And the people believed: and when they heard that the Lord had visited the children of Israel, and that he had looked upon their affliction, then they bowed their heads and worshipped.

2. **Exodus 5:1-23** — And afterward Moses and Aaron went in, and told Pharaoh, Thus saith the Lord God of Israel, Let my people go, that they may hold a feast unto me in the wilderness. And Pharaoh said, Who is the Lord, that I should obey his voice to let Israel go? I know not the Lord, neither will I let Israel go. And they said, The God of the Hebrews hath met with us: let us go, we pray thee, three days' journey into the desert, and sacrifice unto the Lord our God; lest he fall upon us with pestilence, or with the sword. And the king of Egypt said unto them, Wherefore do ye, Moses and Aaron, let the people from their works? get you unto your burdens. And Pharaoh said, Behold, the people of the land now are many, and ye make them rest from their burdens. And Pharaoh commanded the same day the taskmasters of the people, and their officers, saying, Ye shall no more give the people straw to make brick, as heretofore: let them go and gather straw for themselves. And the tale of the bricks, which they did make heretofore, ye shall lay upon them; ye shall not diminish ought thereof: for they be idle; therefore they cry, saying, Let us go and sacrifice to our God. Let there more work be laid upon the men, that they may labour therein; and let them not regard vain words. And the taskmasters of the people went out, and their officers, and they spake to the people, saying, Thus saith Pharaoh, I will not give you straw. Go ye, get you straw where ye can find it: yet not ought of your work shall be diminished. So the people were scattered abroad throughout all the land of Egypt to gather stubble instead of straw. And the taskmasters hasted them, saying, Fulfil your works, your daily tasks, as when there was straw. And the officers of the children of Israel, which Pharaoh's taskmasters had set over them, were beaten, and demanded, Wherefore have ye not fulfilled your task in making brick both yesterday and to day, as heretofore? Then the officers of the children of Israel came and cried unto Pharaoh, saying, Wherefore dealest thou thus with thy servants? There is no straw given unto thy servants, and they say to us, Make brick: and, behold, thy servants are beaten; but the fault

is in thine own people. But he said, Ye are idle, ye are idle: therefore ye say, Let us go and do sacrifice to the Lord. Go therefore now, and work; for there shall no straw be given you, yet shall ye deliver the tale of bricks. And the officers of the children of Israel did see that they were in evil case, after it was said, Ye shall not minish ought from your bricks of your daily task. And they met Moses and Aaron, who stood in the way, as they came forth from Pharaoh: And they said unto them, The Lord look upon you, and judge; because ye have made our savour to be abhorred in the eyes of Pharaoh, and in the eyes of his servants, to put a sword in their hand to slay us. And Moses returned unto the Lord, and said, Lord, wherefore hast thou so evil entreated this people? why is it that thou hast sent me? For since I came to Pharaoh to speak in thy name, he hath done evil to this people; neither hast thou delivered thy people at all.

3. **Exodus 3:19,20** — And I am sure that the king of Egypt will not let you go, no, not by a mighty hand. And I will stretch out my hand, and smite Egypt with all my wonders which I will do in the midst thereof: and after that he will let you go.
4. **Exodus 6:1,5-7,10,11** — Then the Lord said unto Moses, Now shalt thou see what I will do to Pharaoh: for with a strong hand shall he let them go, and with a strong hand shall he drive them out of his land.... And I have also heard the groaning of the children of Israel, whom the Egyptians keep in bondage; and I have remembered my covenant. Wherefore say unto the children of Israel, I am the Lord, and I will bring you out from under the burdens of the Egyptians, and I will rid you out of their bondage, and I will redeem you with a stretched out arm, and with great judgments: And I will take you to me for a people, and I will be to you a God: and ye shall know that I am the Lord your God, which bringeth you out from under the burdens of the Egyptians.... And the Lord spake unto Moses, saying, Go in, speak unto Pharaoh king of Egypt, that he let the children of Israel go out of his land.
5. **Exodus 7:1** — And the Lord said unto Moses, See, I have made thee a god to Pharaoh: and Aaron thy brother shall be thy prophet.

GREEK WORDS

There are no Greek words in this lesson.

SYNOPSIS

Across from the Karnak Temple Complex in Luxor, Egypt, are the royal tombs of the Valley of the Kings. It's located just west of the Nile River in Upper Egypt, and it was part of the ancient city of Thebes. Nearly all of the pharaohs from the Eighteenth, Nineteenth, and Twentieth Egyptian dynasties are entombed there, which includes over five dozen known burial sites. The tomb of King Tut, which was discovered in 1922, is there along with the largest and most complex tomb in the Valley of the Kings — the tomb built for Rameses the Great and all of his sons.

These Egyptian kings lived and ruled the land of Egypt. But there was another person — whose character is larger than life and remembered more than all these kings — named *Moses*. For 40 years, Moses lived in the land of Egypt and was groomed to inherit the throne and serve as one of Egypt's great pharaohs. But after fleeing Egypt and encountering the One True God on Mount Horeb, Moses' life was forever changed.

Although Moses would have never imagined returning to the land of Egypt after he left, that is exactly what God had him do. At 80 years of age, God sent him straight into the heart of the beast — to Pharaoh himself — to deliver his people, the children of Israel, from Egyptian bondage.

The emphasis of this lesson:

Moses' first confrontation with Pharaoh made things worse for the children of Israel, not better. Pharaoh forced the Hebrews to go and get their own straw for making bricks, and as a result, the Israelites had great contempt for Moses and Aaron. Yet God reassured Moses and the Israelites He would set them free from Egyptian bondage with a mighty hand, and He would make them His very own people.

Moses Received Jethro's Blessing and Then Went With Aaron To Meet With the Elders of Israel

Before Moses returned to Egypt to deliver Israel from bondage, the Bible says he first, "…went and returned to Jethro his father in law, and said unto him, Let me go, I pray thee, and return unto my brethren which are in Egypt, and see whether they be yet alive. And Jethro said to Moses, Go in peace" (Exodus 4:18).

Moses was to *obey* and do exactly what God told him to do. But because he had been submitted to Jethro's spiritual authority for nearly 40 years, he set the example of returning to Jethro before he launched out. Even Moses was submitted to spiritual authority, and the Bible shows us that Jethro's role remained strong in Moses' life for years to come.

Scripture goes on to say, "And the Lord said unto Moses in Midian, Go, return into Egypt: for all the men are dead which sought thy life. And Moses took his wife and his sons, and set them upon an ass, and he returned to the land of Egypt: and Moses took the rod of God in his hand. And the Lord said unto Moses, When thou goest to return into Egypt, see that thou do all those wonders before Pharaoh, which I have put in thine hand..." (Exodus 4:19-21).

Moses then met Aaron in the wilderness and shared with him all that God had said. Together, they went and gathered all the elders of Israel and told them what God had said and performed the signs the Lord had given to Moses on Mount Horeb. The elders believed Moses and were deeply moved by God's awareness of their affliction and worshiped God upon hearing the news of their deliverance (*see* Exodus 4:27-31).

Moses' First Confrontation With Pharaoh

Looking at Exodus 5:1, the Bible says, "And afterward Moses and Aaron went in, and told Pharaoh, Thus saith the Lord God of Israel, Let my people go, that they may hold a feast unto me in the wilderness." Through His messengers, Moses and Aaron, God demanded that Pharaoh give freedom to His people.

This confrontation took tremendous courage. Again, in the Egyptians' eyes, Pharaoh was viewed as more than a man. He was believed to be a god and a friend to the greatest gods of Egypt. Each Pharaoh sat with these gods in their own temples and received worship alongside them. The Pharaoh's power and authority were supreme, and there was no law, no legislature, and no constitution equal to him.

Having grown up in the royal courts of Egypt, Moses was very familiar with this dynamic, and he knew that Pharaoh was just a mortal man.

Therefore, Moses came solely on the authority of the living God, and he confronted Pharaoh with God's demands.

To this Pharaoh responded, "...*Who is the Lord*, that I should obey his voice to let Israel go? I know not the Lord, neither will I let Israel go" (Exodus 5:2). Pharaoh knew of many gods, but he didn't know about the Hebrew God Yahweh. In just a short time, he was going to get a crash course introduction to the God he never knew.

Moses and Aaron then said, "...The God of the Hebrews hath met with us: let us go, we pray thee, three days' journey into the desert, and sacrifice unto the Lord our God; lest he fall upon us with pestilence, or with the sword. And the king of Egypt said unto them, Wherefore do ye, Moses and Aaron, let the people from their works? get you unto your burdens" (Exodus 5:3,4). Immediately, Pharaoh rejected God's command to let the Israelites go and worship God, seeing it as nothing more than a waste of good working time.

Things Got Worse Before They Got Better

Pharaoh continued by saying, "...Behold, the people of the land now are many, and ye make them rest from their burdens. And Pharaoh commanded the same day the taskmasters of the people, and their officers, saying, Ye shall no more give the people straw to make brick, as heretofore: let them go and gather straw for themselves. And the tale of the bricks, which they did make heretofore, ye shall lay upon them; ye shall not diminish ought thereof: for they be idle; therefore they cry, saying, Let us go and sacrifice to our God" (Exodus 5:5-8).

Pharaoh's command to the taskmasters to no longer provide straw for making bricks was intended to punish Israel for the request — and to give them more work. Straw made bricks stronger. In the process of making bricks, straw was chopped and mixed into the clay, making the bricks stronger by first binding the clay together and then drying the bricks in the sun. The use of straw in making bricks in Egypt during this period is confirmed by archaeology. Bricks of all sorts have been found in Egypt, some with regularly chopped straw, and some without straw. What is most interesting is that there are more bricks from the Thutmose period than any other period, and many of them were made *without* straw just as the Bible says!

Persisting in his rant, Pharaoh said, "Let there more work be laid upon the men, that they may labour therein; and let them not regard vain words" (Exodus 5:9). The "vain words" referred to here was the idea of going out into the wilderness to worship God for three days. In Pharaoh's mind, more work would get such nonsense off the minds of the Hebrew slaves.

Meanwhile, the Bible says, "And the taskmasters of the people went out, and their officers, and they spake to the people, saying, Thus saith Pharaoh, I will not give you straw. Go ye, get you straw where ye can find it: yet not ought of your work shall be diminished. So the people were scattered abroad throughout all the land of Egypt to gather stubble instead of straw. And the taskmasters hasted them, saying, Fulfil your works, your daily tasks, as when there was straw" (Exodus 5:10-13).

The immediate effects of the first request of God to deliver the children of Israel from Egypt made conditions worse for all the Hebrews. The Bible says, "And the officers of the children of Israel, which Pharaoh's taskmasters had set over them, were beaten, and demanded, Wherefore have ye not fulfilled your task in making brick both yesterday and to day, as heretofore?" (Exodus 5:14)

The Israelites Cried to Pharaoh and Held Contempt for Moses and Aaron

Exodus 5:15 and 16 says, "Then the officers of the children of Israel came and cried unto Pharaoh, saying, Wherefore dealest thou thus with thy servants? There is no straw given unto thy servants, and they say to us, Make brick: and, behold, thy servants are beaten; but the fault is in thine own people."

Here we see the officers of the children of Israel *crying* to Pharaoh — just as all the Hebrews had *cried out* to God because of their bondage (*see* Exodus 2:23). This is one of the two things we noted that God hears from Heaven: He hears the *cries of His people* and the *cry of sin* in the earth (*see* Genesis 18:20,21). Once these cries reach a maximum point, He comes down and responds.

Clearly, Pharaoh was a cruel, wicked tyrant. He believed the Israelites were lazy and that more work — and *harder work* — would cure them of laziness. This is why he responded by saying, "...Ye are idle, ye are idle: therefore ye say, Let us go and do sacrifice to the Lord. Go therefore now, and work; for there shall no straw be given you, yet shall ye deliver the tale of bricks. And the officers of the children of Israel saw that they were in an evil case, after it was said, Ye shall not minish ought from your bricks of your daily task" (Exodus 5:17-19).

As the Hebrew officers were leaving Pharaoh's chambers, the Bible says, "And they met Moses and Aaron, who stood in the way, as they came forth from Pharaoh: And they said unto them, The Lord look upon you, and judge; because ye have made our savour to be abhorred in the eyes of Pharaoh, and in the eyes of his servants, to put a sword in their hand to slay us" (Exodus 5:20,21).

Clearly, the leaders of the children of Israel were not happy with Moses and Aaron. They believed all of their new misery was a direct result of these two men's actions. Consequently, Israel's leaders had contempt for Moses and Aaron from the start.

Moses Voiced His Frustration to the Lord

At that point, Moses was overwhelmed and frustrated by what had happened. Scripture says, "And Moses returned unto the Lord, and said, Lord, wherefore hast thou so evil entreated this people? why is it that thou hast sent me? For since I came to Pharaoh to speak in thy name, he hath done evil to this people; neither hast thou delivered thy people at all" (Exodus 5:22,23).

Although Moses did well to speak so boldly to God, it appears from these verses that he had probably forgotten what God told him at the burning bush — specifically, that Pharaoh would *not* easily let the Israelites go. Remember, Exodus 3:19 says, "And I [God] am sure that the king of Egypt will not let you go, *no, not by a mighty hand*," which in Hebrew means "**except** by a mighty hand." God then declared, "And I will stretch out my hand, and smite Egypt with all my wonders which I will do in the midst thereof: and after that he will let you go" (Exodus 3:20).

More than likely, as Moses lay there on the ground alone before God, he was probably wishing he was back in Midian. After being humbled for 40 years, learning to herd his father-in-law's sheep, he probably thought that dying to himself was done. But now in the new circumstances in which he found himself, he had to die to himself yet again. This is the crucifixion of the flesh the apostle Paul talks about in Galatians 2:20 — it is a process that never ends.

Although Moses was caught off guard by the chain of events, God was not. He knew exactly how Pharaoh would respond, which is why he tried to prepare Moses in advance. If you run into unexpected challenges on your way to fulfilling your God-assignment, think back to what God spoke to you, and be assured that He is not surprised.

God Reassured Moses of His Powerful Plan To Rescue Israel and Bring Judgment on Egypt

In His kindness and mercy, the Lord responded to Moses and calmed his heart and mind. With great boldness, He declared, "...Now shalt thou see what I will do to Pharaoh: for with a strong hand shall he let them [the children of Israel] go, and with a strong hand shall he drive them out of his land" (Exodus 6:1). Essentially, God said, "By the time I'm finished with Pharaoh, he will be thrilled for the children of Israel to leave. In fact, he will drive them out of Egypt with a strong hand."

God then reassured Moses that He was aware of what was going on. He said, "And I have also heard the groaning of the children of Israel, whom the Egyptians keep in bondage; and I have remembered my covenant. Wherefore say unto the children of Israel, I am the Lord, and I will bring you out from under the burdens of the Egyptians, and I will rid you out of their bondage, and I will redeem you with a stretched out arm, and with great judgments: And I will take you to me for a people, and I will be to you a God: and ye shall know that I am the Lord your God, which bringeth you out from under the burdens of the Egyptians" (Exodus 6:5-7).

God Made Five 'I WILL' Promises to Moses and Israel

1. I will bring you out from under the burdens of the Egyptians.
2. I will rid you from their bondage.
3. I will redeem you with an outstretched arm and great judgments.
4. I will take you to me a people.
5. I will be to you a God.

What's truly amazing is that each of these verbs used in Exodus 6:6 and 7 are in the Hebrew past tense. This means God was so certain these things would happen that He viewed them as having already been completed!

Moses Stood in the Place of God Before Pharaoh

The Scripture goes on to say, "And the Lord spake unto Moses, saying, Go in, speak unto Pharaoh king of Egypt, that he let the children of Israel go out of his land.... And the Lord said unto Moses, See, I have made thee a god to Pharaoh: and Aaron thy brother shall be thy prophet" (Exodus 6:10,11; 7:1).

God knew that what He was about to do through Moses was going to elevate him in Pharaoh's eyes to the status of a god. Each time Moses would stand before Pharaoh, he would stand in the place of God and speak on God's behalf. Eventually, Pharaoh would tremble in the presence of Moses.

The truth is, that's the position of every preacher and teacher of God's Word. They stand in the place of God and speak on His behalf. Thus, the pulpit belongs to God, not us. And we're not only to deliver God's message, but also to do it with the power of the Holy Spirit. It's the Spirit's power that demonstrates the authority of the message and authenticates that we are sent by God.

How Did Pharaoh Respond to Moses?

God went on to tell Moses, "And I will harden Pharaoh's heart, and multiply my signs and my wonders in the land of Egypt. But Pharaoh shall not hearken unto you, that I may lay my hand upon Egypt, and bring forth mine armies, and my people the children of Israel, out of the land of Egypt by great judgments. And the Egyptians shall know that I am the Lord, when I stretch forth mine hand upon Egypt, and bring out the children of Israel from among them" (Exodus 7:3-5).

God was determined He was going to punish Egypt for what they had done to His people. At the same time, He was going to make sure He fully answered Pharaoh's question and let him know *who the Lord is*! Again and again, God would stretch forth His hand using the rod in Moses' hand and bring great judgments — in the form of plagues — upon Egypt.

There's something else important that you need to see. These wonders God was about to perform would give the people of Egypt an opportunity to repent and acknowledge God as the One True God. We know from Scripture that a number of Egyptians did repent. Exodus 12:38 says, "And a mixed multitude went up also with them; and flocks, and herds, even very much cattle."

According to Exodus 7:6, "...Moses and Aaron did as the Lord commanded them...." God sent them to Pharaoh and they did precisely what they were told to do. Their obedience to God and their faith in His word released His dynamic power. Friend, if the assignment God has given you seems difficult, know that you're not alone! Just as God was with Moses, He is with you. And as you step out in faith and obey His instructions, His powerful anointing will manifest in your situation.

STUDY QUESTIONS

Study to shew thyself approved unto God, a workman that needeth not to be ashamed, rightly dividing the word of truth.
— 2 Timothy 2:15

1. Before heading out to accomplish the task God had given him, Moses returned to his father-in-law Jethro, submitted to his authority, and asked for his blessing to be released and return to Egypt. If Moses — who received direction straight from God — was submitted to Jethro, what does that say to you about submitting to authority? Whose authority are you submitted to?
2. The five "I WILL" promises God made to Moses and the children of Israel are all written in *past tense*, which means in God's mind, their deliverance was already a done deal. What verses can you think of in Scripture that declare you're already victorious over the enemy?
3. Take a few moments to look up and write down these powerful promises that proclaim your position of victory in Christ:
   - Luke 10:19
   - Romans 8:37
   - 2 Corinthians 2:14
   - John 16:33
   - 1 John 5:4

PRACTICAL APPLICATION

But be ye doers of the word, and not hearers only,
deceiving your own selves.
—James 1:22

The immediate effects of God beginning the process of deliverance for the Israelites made matters worse. The workers were forced to make bricks without straw, and the Hebrew team leaders were beaten when the tally of bricks fell short. Stop and think:

1. If you were *Moses*, how would you have responded?
2. If you were one of the *Hebrew officers*, how do you think you would have reacted to being beaten?
3. If you were a *common worker*, what might have been your reaction to having to get your own straw to make bricks?
4. Have you ever experienced a situation like this in which things seemed to get worse instead of better? If so, briefly share what took place. How does this biblical example help you see things differently?

LESSON 7

TOPIC

Plagues of Blood, Frogs, and Lice

SCRIPTURES

1. **Exodus 5:2** — And Pharaoh said, Who is the Lord, that I should obey His voice to let Israel go?
2. **Exodus 7:2-25** — Thou shalt speak all that I command thee: and Aaron thy brother shall speak unto Pharaoh, that he send the children of Israel out of his land. And I will harden Pharaoh's heart, and multiply my signs and my wonders in the land of Egypt. But Pharaoh shall not hearken unto you, that I may lay my hand upon Egypt, and bring forth mine armies, and my people the children of Israel, out of the land of Egypt by great judgments. And the Egyptians shall know that I am the Lord, when I stretch forth mine hand upon Egypt, and bring out the children of Israel from among them. And Moses and Aaron

did as the Lord commanded them, so did they.... And the Lord spake unto Moses and unto Aaron, saying, When Pharaoh shall speak unto you, saying, Shew a miracle for you: then thou shalt say unto Aaron, Take thy rod, and cast it before Pharaoh, and it shall become a serpent. And Moses and Aaron went in unto Pharaoh, and they did so as the Lord had commanded: and Aaron cast down his rod before Pharaoh, and before his servants, and it became a serpent. Then Pharaoh also called the wise men and the sorcerers: now the magicians of Egypt, they also did in like manner with their enchantments. For they cast down every man his rod, and they became serpents: but Aaron's rod swallowed up their rods... And the Lord said unto Moses, Pharaoh's heart is hardened, he refuseth to let the people go. Get thee unto Pharaoh in the morning; lo, he goeth out unto the water; and thou shalt stand by the river's brink against he come; and the rod which was turned to a serpent shalt thou take in thine hand. And thou shalt say unto him, The Lord God of the Hebrews hath sent me unto thee, saying, Let my people go, that they may serve me in the wilderness: and, behold, hitherto thou wouldest not hear. Thus saith the Lord, In this thou shalt know that I am the Lord: behold, I will smite with the rod that is in mine hand upon the waters which are in the river, and they shall be turned to blood. And the fish that is in the river shall die, and the river shall stink; and the Egyptians shall lothe to drink of the water of the river. And the Lord spake unto Moses, Say unto Aaron, Take thy rod, and stretch out thine hand upon the waters of Egypt, upon their streams, upon their rivers, and upon their ponds, and upon all their pools of water, that they may become blood; and that there may be blood throughout all the land of Egypt, both in vessels of wood, and in vessels of stone. And Moses and Aaron did so, as the Lord commanded; and he lifted up the rod, and smote the waters that were in the river, in the sight of Pharaoh, and in the sight of his servants; and all the waters that were in the river were turned to blood. And the fish that was in the river died; and the river stank, and the Egyptians could not drink of the water of the river; and there was blood throughout all the land of Egypt. And the magicians of Egypt did so with their enchantments: and Pharaoh's heart was hardened, neither did he hearken unto them; as the Lord had said. And Pharaoh turned and went into his house, neither did he set his heart to this also. And all the Egyptians digged round about the river for water to drink; for they could not drink of the water of the river. And seven days were fulfilled, after that the Lord had smitten the river.

3. **Exodus 8:1-19** — And the Lord spake unto Moses, Go unto Pharaoh, and say unto him, Thus saith the Lord, Let my people go, that they may serve me. And if thou refuse to let them go, behold, I will smite all thy borders with frogs: And the river shall bring forth frogs abundantly, which shall go up and come into thine house, and into thy bedchamber, and upon thy bed, and into the house of thy servants, and upon thy people, and into thine ovens, and into thy kneadingtroughs: And the frogs shall come up both on thee, and upon thy people, and upon all thy servants. And the Lord spake unto Moses, Say unto Aaron, Stretch forth thine hand with thy rod over the streams, over the rivers, and over the ponds, and cause frogs to come up upon the land of Egypt. And Aaron stretched out his hand over the waters of Egypt; and the frogs came up, and covered the land of Egypt. And the magicians did so with their enchantments, and brought up frogs upon the land of Egypt. Then Pharaoh called for Moses and Aaron, and said, Intreat the Lord, that he may take away the frogs from me, and from my people; and I will let the people go, that they may do sacrifice unto the Lord. And Moses said unto Pharaoh, Glory over me: when shall I intreat for thee, and for thy servants, and for thy people, to destroy the frogs from thee and thy houses, that they may remain in the river only? And he said, To morrow. And he said, Be it according to thy word: that thou mayest know that there is none like unto the Lord our God. And the frogs shall depart from thee, and from thy houses, and from thy servants, and from thy people; they shall remain in the river only. And Moses and Aaron went out from Pharaoh: and Moses cried unto the Lord because of the frogs which he had brought against Pharaoh. And the Lord did according to the word of Moses; and the frogs died out of the houses, out of the villages, and out of the fields. And they gathered them together upon heaps: and the land stank. But when Pharaoh saw that there was respite, he hardened his heart, and hearkened not unto them; as the Lord had said. And the Lord said unto Moses, Say unto Aaron, Stretch out thy rod, and smite the dust of the land, that it may become lice throughout all the land of Egypt. And they did so; for Aaron stretched out his hand with his rod, and smote the dust of the earth, and it became lice in man, and in beast; all the dust of the land became lice throughout all the land of Egypt. And the magicians

did so with their enchantments to bring forth lice, but they could not: so there were lice upon man, and upon beast. Then the magicians said unto Pharaoh, This is the finger of God: and Pharaoh's heart was hardened, and he hearkened not unto them; as the Lord had said.

GREEK WORDS

There are no Greek words in this lesson.

SYNOPSIS

The New Hermitage Museum in Saint Petersburg, Russia, is an enormous complex that features 2,511,000 square feet of history on display. Every square inch of its interior is filled with rich treasures — including a massive room dedicated to ancient Egyptian history.

If you were to board a ship and travel up the Nile River in Egypt, you would see with your own eyes many of the same sites and structures that Moses and the children Israel saw in their day. These include the legendary Sphinx of Giza, the ancient pyramids, the temple cities of Karnak and Luxor, the Valley of the Kings, and a unique temple at Kom Ombo dedicated to Sobek, the crocodile god.

When the cries of the Hebrew nation reached the ears of God in Heaven, He raised up Moses to deliver His people from the Egyptian taskmasters and the tyrannical rule of Pharaoh. God's weapons of mass destruction were manifested in the form of ten powerful plagues — each one uniquely designed to humiliate the gods of Egypt and utterly destroy the land's riches and resources.

The emphasis of this lesson:

When Moses' rod became a serpent and swallowed up the magicians' serpents (rods), God prophetically foretold that Egypt's power and protection would be swallowed up by God's power. The first plague He brought against Egypt was to turn the waters of the Nile into blood. He quickly followed this plague with an invasion of frogs and an infestation of lice.

God Declared He Would Demonstrate His Superiority Over All the Gods of Egypt

As Exodus 7 begins, God is speaking with Moses, urging him to speak everything He has commanded and to demand that Pharaoh let the children of Israel go. Knowing in advance that Pharaoh would not listen to Moses, God declared, "…I [will] lay my hand upon Egypt, and bring forth mine armies, and my people the children of Israel, out of the land of Egypt by great judgments. And the Egyptians shall know that I am the Lord, when I stretch forth mine hand upon Egypt, and bring out the children of Israel from among them" (Exodus 7:4,5). The Egyptians had beaten the Israelites with rods, and now God was going to stretch forth His hand and let Egypt know how it feels to be beaten.

What's interesting is that as you read through the series of ten plagues God unleashed on the Egyptians, there was a space of time between each one. Although the exact amount of time is not known, we do know there was enough time to allow a number of the Egyptians to repent and surrender themselves to the Lord, recognizing Him as the One True God. Exodus 12:38 confirms this fact, informing us that there was a "mixed multitude" that left Egypt when Israel was brought out.

Remember, in Exodus 5:2 Pharaoh sneeringly asked the question. "Who is the Lord…?" Now God was going to answer his question by unequivocally demonstrating that He is greater than…

- The god **Hapi** (the spirit of the Nile)
- The god **Khnum** (the guardian of the Nile)
- The god **Osiris** (who had the Nile as his bloodstream)
- The goddess **Heket** (the frog-goddess of fertility)
- The goddess **Hathor** (a cow-like mother goddess)
- The god **Imhotep** (the god of medicine)
- The goddess **Nut** (the sky goddess)

What did Moses and Aaron do with God's instructions? The Bible says, "And Moses and Aaron did as the Lord commanded them, so did they" (Exodus 7:6).

Egypt's Power and Protection Would Be Swallowed Up by God's Power

Scripture goes on to say, "And the Lord spake unto Moses and unto Aaron, saying, When Pharaoh shall speak unto you, saying, Shew a miracle for you: then thou shalt say unto Aaron, Take thy rod, and cast it before Pharaoh, and it shall become a serpent. And Moses and Aaron went in unto Pharaoh, and they did so as the Lord had commanded: and Aaron cast down his rod before Pharaoh, and before his servants, and it became a serpent" (Exodus 7:8-10). As we noted previously, it was believed that the serpent — specifically the cobra — was a symbol of promised protection and power from the gods for Pharaoh and his successors. The fact that Moses now held such power in the rod of his hand spoke volumes to the Egyptians.

Responding to this extraordinary display, Scripture says, "Then Pharaoh also called the wise men and the sorcerers: now the magicians of Egypt, they also did in like manner with their enchantments. For they cast down every man his rod, and they became serpents..." (Exodus 7:11,12). According to Second Timothy 3:8, two of the leading Egyptian magicians that stood against Moses were Jannes and Jambres, and they were able to duplicate the sign he did.

Occult phenomena was widespread in Egypt. The Egyptian magicians were famous occult priests that were known to conjure up and utilize demonic power. It has been said by some scholars that these magicians were so immersed in satanic power that they had the ability to take a serpent and so hypnotize it that it became as stiff as a rod. Thus, the "rods" in the hands of the magicians that became snakes were believed to already have been serpents that were released from the spell cast on them.

In any case, the Bible says, "...Aaron's rod swallowed up their rods" (Exodus 7:12). This was God's way of telling Pharaoh and the people of Egypt, "I don't care how much power you think you possess or how many tricks you have up your sleeves. I am going to swallow up all of Egypt's power and protection."

Josephus wrote about this particular incident, saying:

> ...The king very angry... commanded the priests to let him see the same wonderful sights; as knowing that the Egyptians were

skillful in this kind of learning... Now when the priests threw down their rods, they became serpents. But Moses was not daunted at it; and said... 'That what I do, is so much superior to what these do by magic arts and tricks, as Divine power exceeds the power of man: but I will demonstrate that what I do is not done by craft, or counterfeiting what is not really true; but that they appear by the providence and power of God.' And when he had said this, he cast his rod down upon the ground, and commanded it to turn itself into a serpent. It obeyed him, and went all round, and devoured the rods of the Egyptians, which seemed to be dragons, until it had consumed them all. It then returned to its own form, and Moses took it into his hand again.[1]

But when the King despised the words of Moses, and had no regard at all to them, grievous plagues seized the Egyptians... no such plagues did ever happen to any other nation as the Egyptians now felt....[2]

Plague #1: *God Turned the Waters to Blood*

The Nile and All Its Tributaries Became Blood

Although you might think Pharaoh would listen to the voice of God, he did not. Instead, the Bible says, "And the Lord said unto Moses, Pharaoh's heart is hardened, he refuseth to let the people go. Get thee unto Pharaoh in the morning; lo, he goeth out unto the water; and thou shalt stand by the river's brink against he come; and the rod which was turned to a serpent shalt thou take in thine hand. And thou shalt say unto him, The Lord God of the Hebrews hath sent me unto thee, saying, Let my people go, that they may serve me in the wilderness: and, behold, hitherto thou wouldest not hear. Thus saith the Lord, In this thou shalt know that I am the Lord: behold, I will smite with the rod that is in mine hand upon the waters which are in the river, and they shall be turned to blood. And the fish that is in the river shall die, and the river shall stink; and the Egyptians shall lothe to drink of the water of the river" (Exodus 7:14-18).

Isn't it interesting that Moses said that the rod in "mine hand" would smite the waters and they would turn to blood? This means in that moment, Moses' hand became God's hand! This reveals how God uses men and women who are yielded to Him as His instruments to accomplish His will on the earth. Turning the Nile River and the waters of Egypt into blood was the first of the ten plagues.

Exodus 7:19-21 goes on to say, "And the Lord spake unto Moses, Say unto Aaron, Take thy rod, and stretch out thine hand upon the waters of Egypt, upon their streams, upon their rivers, and upon their ponds, and upon all their pools of water, that they may become blood; and that there may be blood throughout all the land of Egypt, both in vessels of wood, and in vessels of stone. And Moses and Aaron did so, as the Lord commanded; and he lifted up the rod, and smote the waters that were in the river, in the sight of Pharaoh, and in the sight of his servants; and all the waters that were in the river were turned to blood. And the fish that was in the river died; and the river stank, and the Egyptians could not drink of the water of the river; and there was blood throughout all the land of Egypt."

Each Plague Was Literal, Not Figurative and They Struck Down the Gods of Egypt

It's important to understand that these plagues were all literal and not metaphorical. Each of the plagues confronted and assaulted an Egyptian deity and was designed by God to answer Pharaoh's original question: "Who is the Lord, that I should obey His voice to let Israel go?" (Exodus 5:2). These plagues show that *Yahweh* is greater than any of the gods of Egypt.

The word "plagues" means *blow* or *strike*. Each plague was as if God was *striking* or *beating* a deity worshiped by the Egyptians. For instance, this first plague was directed against the Egyptian river and its deities. Remember, the Nile itself was worshiped as a god by the Egyptians and seen as the birthplace of the gods.

By turning the waters to blood, God showed that He has complete power over...

- The god **Hapi**: he was believed to be the spirit of the Nile and was humiliated by this strike on the waters.
- The god **Khnum**: he was reputedly the guardian of the Nile, and this showed he was incapable of providing protection.
- The god **Osiris**: he was believed to have the Nile as his bloodstream, and through this blow upon the Nile, Osiris blood appeared to flow endlessly.

Once the Nile was filled with blood, it became undrinkable. This was an abomination in the site of the Egyptians, and there was nothing they could do to stop it.

The Egyptian Magicians Were Able To Turn Water Into Blood

Interestingly, just as the Egyptian sorcerers duplicated the wonder of turning their rods into serpents, the Bible says, "And the magicians of Egypt did so [to the waters of the Nile] with their enchantments: and Pharaoh's heart was hardened, neither did he hearken unto them; as the Lord had said" (Exodus 7:22). Apparently, after the Egyptians dug around the river to find fresh water to drink (*see* Exodus 7:24), the magicians took some of this fresh water and turned it into blood.

If you think about it, if the magicians really wanted to show that their power was greater than the power of God, they would have turned the bloody waters of the Nile back into healthy, drinkable water. But they couldn't because the power they were operating under was Satan's, and he is unable to perform anything good or constructive. All he can do is pervert and destroy what God creates.

Josephus weighed in on the water turning to blood saying:

> For the Egyptian river ran with bloody water at the command of God; insomuch that it could not be drunk, and they had no other spring of water neither; For the water was not only of the color of blood, but it brought upon those that ventured to drink of it great pains, and bitter torment. Such was the river to the Egyptians; but it was sweet and fit for drinking to the Hebrews, and no way different from what it naturally used to be… (the king) gave the Hebrews leave to go away. But when the plague ceased, he changed his mind again, and would not suffer them to go.[3]

The seventh chapter of Exodus closes by saying, "And Pharaoh turned and went into his house, neither did he set his heart to this also…. And seven days were fulfilled, after that the Lord had smitten the river" (Exodus 7:23,25).

Plague #2: *God Caused a Massive Invasion of Frogs*

Why Frogs?

The eighth chapter of Exodus opens with God speaking to Moses and saying, "…Go unto Pharaoh, and say unto him, Thus saith the Lord, Let my people go, that they may serve me. And if thou refuse to let them go, behold, I will smite all thy borders with frogs" (Exodus 8:1,2). There are a couple of words worth noting here. First is the word "behold," which basically means, *Wow! You better get ready! Something huge is coming!*

Next, notice the phrase "I will smite." This is the equivalent of the Lord saying, "I am going to afflict." God threatened to *afflict* or *greatly trouble* all the territory of Egypt with frogs. Why frogs? It's because one of the Egyptian gods — the god Heket — was always pictured with the head of a frog. Heket was believed to be a goddess of fertility. Thus, frogs were a sacred symbol of an Egyptian god, and therefore, they could not be killed. The plague of frogs was a direct attack on the god Heket.

The Lord then told Moses to tell Pharaoh, "And the river shall bring forth frogs abundantly, which shall go up and come into thine house, and into thy bedchamber, and upon thy bed, and into the house of thy servants, and upon thy people, and into thine ovens, and into thy kneadingtroughs: And the frogs shall come up both on thee, and upon thy people, and upon all thy servants. And the Lord spake unto Moses, Say unto Aaron, Stretch forth thine hand with thy rod over the streams, over the rivers, and over the ponds, and cause frogs to come up upon the land of Egypt. And Aaron stretched out his hand over the waters of Egypt; and the frogs came up, and covered the land of Egypt" (Exodus 8:3-6).

Sure enough, the frogs came up and covered the entire land of Egypt. Since the Egyptians wanted to worship the frog, God gave them a plethora of frogs.

Regarding this second plague, Josephus wrote:

> …He sent another plague upon the Egyptians: An innumerable multitude of frogs consumed the fruit of the ground; The river was also full of them, insomuch that those who drew water had it spoiled by the blood of these animals, as they died in, and were destroyed by the water; and the country was full of filthy slime… they also spoiled their vessels in their houses which they used, and

> were found among what they ate and what they drank, and came in great numbers upon their beds.[4]

Exodus 8:7 says, "And the magicians did so with their enchantments, and brought up frogs upon the land of Egypt." Once again, as with turning the fresh well water into blood, the magicians ridiculously made more frogs! Instead of getting rid of the frogs and fixing the problem, they only made it worse.

The Dead Frogs Produced a Nauseating Stench

Scripture says, "Then Pharaoh called for Moses and Aaron, and said, Intreat the Lord, that he may take away the frogs from me, and from my people; and I will let the people go, that they may do sacrifice unto the Lord" (Exodus 8:8). When Pharaoh said, "Intreat the Lord," he was urging Moses to *pray* and *intercede* to God for him. Remember, Pharaoh and all the other Egyptians couldn't lift a finger to harm a frog because they were sacred to them. That's why Pharaoh begged Moses to ask God to remove them.

Moses answered Pharaoh and said, "...Glory over me: when shall I intreat for thee, and for thy servants, and for thy people, to destroy the frogs from thee and thy houses, that they may remain in the river only? And he said, To morrow. And he said, Be it according to thy word: that thou mayest know that there is none like unto the Lord our God. And the frogs shall depart from thee, and from thy houses, and from thy servants, and from thy people; they shall remain in the river only. And Moses and Aaron went out from Pharaoh: and Moses cried unto the Lord because of the frogs which he had brought against Pharaoh. And the Lord did according to the word of Moses; and the frogs died out of the houses, out of the villages, and out of the fields. And they gathered them together upon heaps: and the land stank" (Exodus 8:9-14).

So Moses prayed, God answered, and all the frogs died. The fact that the Bible says "the land stank" gives a hint at how nauseating the smell must have been. *Now* you would think that Pharaoh would honor his word and let the Israelites go as he said he would. Yet Exodus 8:15 says, "But when Pharaoh saw that there was respite, he hardened his heart, and hearkened not unto them; as the Lord had said."

Plague #3: *God Created an Infestation of Lice*

The First Sign the Magicians Couldn't Duplicate

Leaving no time for the dust to settle after the second plague, God advanced to plague number 3. This plague would come upon Egypt unannounced and without warning. Exodus 8:16 says, "And the Lord said unto Moses, Say unto Aaron, Stretch out thy rod, and smite the dust of the land, that it may become lice throughout all the land of Egypt."

Stop and think about how much dust — or sand — there is in the land of Egypt. It's everywhere! That means when Moses obeyed God and had Aaron strike the dust of the ground, God turned every particle into lice. Every place the people walked they were walking through lice. This plague struck a hard blow to the heart of Egyptian religion — particularly the priesthood. They were always very concerned with ritualistic cleansing and hygiene. The infestation of lice made it impossible to worship their gods due to their uncleanness.

The Bible says when Aaron stretched out his hand with his rod and smote the dust of the earth, "...it became lice in man, and in beast; all the dust of the land became lice throughout all the land of Egypt" (Exodus 8:17). And unlike the two previous plagues, the Bible says, "And the magicians did so with their enchantments to bring forth lice, but they could not: so there were lice upon man, and upon beast" (Exodus 8:18). Note that this plague of lice was also upon *every beast*. This means the Egyptian priests' sacrifices were stopped because they could not offer a sacrifice of lice-infested animals to their gods.

Moved by this powerful plague, "...The magicians said unto Pharaoh, This is the finger of God: and Pharaoh's heart was hardened, and he hearkened not unto them; as the Lord had said" (Exodus 8:19).

Josephus wrote about the infestation of lice and said:

> Accordingly, God punished his [Pharaoh's] falseness with another plague, added to the former; for there arose out of the bodies of the Egyptian an innumerable quantity of lice, by which, wicked as they were, they miserably perished, as not able to destroy this sort of vermin either with washes or with ointments.[5]

There was nothing the Egyptians could do to get rid of the lice. Only God could remove them. Pharaoh and his people were finding out firsthand who the Lord is and that He is greater and more powerful than all the gods of Egypt. In our next lesson, we will focus on the next three plagues God brought upon Egypt: *the swarms of flies, disease on the livestock, and the boils.*

STUDY QUESTIONS

Study to shew thyself approved unto God, a workman that needeth not to be ashamed, rightly dividing the word of truth.
— 2 Timothy 2:15

1. The word "plague" means *to blow* or *to strike*. Each plague that God brought against the Egyptians was a direct attack on the gods of Egypt. What new insights did you learn about the Nile River and the deities that were connected with it? How about Heket — the frog-like goddess of fertility?
2. God is a God of justice. He repaid the Egyptians for their wretched abuse of His people and at the same time reimbursed Israel all the wages they earned for their labors. What does God say about paying *you* back for your efforts and taking care of your enemies? Consider these promises He's made to you:
   - 2 Samuel 22:21,25-27
   - Proverbs 11:31
   - 2 Thessalonians 1:6,7
   - Hebrews 10:35,36

PRACTICAL APPLICATION

But be ye doers of the word, and not hearers only, deceiving your own selves.
—James 1:22

Again and again throughout the story of Moses and the ten plagues, we hear the phrases: "Pharaoh hardened his heart"; "Pharaoh's heart was hardened"; and "God hardened Pharaoh's heart." If you were Moses and you had had a burning-bush encounter with God and you knew it was God's will to deliver Israel…

1. How do you think you would have handled Pharaoh continually hardening his heart against what God said?
2. How would you have responded knowing that at times it was *God* Himself who was doing the hardening (*see* Exodus7:3-5)?
3. What was God's greater purpose in this? (Consider Exodus 3:19-22; 6:1; 7:3-5.)
4. How does this help you see your current difficulties in a better light?

---

[1] Flavius Josephus, "The Words of Flavius Josephus: Translated by William Whiston; Antiquities of the Jews," Book II, chap. 13.3.

[2] Flavius Josephus, "The Words of Flavius Josephus: Translated by William Whiston; Antiquities of the Jews," Book II, chap. 14.1.

[3] Flavius Josephus, "The Words of Flavius Josephus: Translated by William Whiston; Antiquities of the Jews," Book II, chap. 14.1.

[4] Flavius Josephus, "The Words of Flavius Josephus: Translated by William Whiston; Antiquities of the Jews," Book II, chap. 14.2.

[5] Flavius Josephus, "The Words of Flavius Josephus: Translated by William Whiston; Antiquities of the Jews," Book II, chap. 14.3.

LESSON 8

TOPIC

Plagues of Flies, Disease, and Boils

SCRIPTURES

1. **Exodus 8:20-32** — And the Lord said unto Moses, Rise up early in the morning, and stand before Pharaoh; lo, he cometh forth to the water; and say unto him, Thus saith the Lord, Let my people go, that they may serve me. Else, if thou wilt not let my people go, behold, I will send swarms of flies upon thee, and upon thy servants, and upon thy people, and into thy houses: and the houses of the Egyptians shall be full of swarms of flies, and also the ground whereon they are. And I will sever in that day the land of Goshen, in which my people dwell, that no swarms of flies shall be there; to the end thou mayest know

that I am the Lord in the midst of the earth. And I will put a division between my people and thy people: to morrow shall this sign be. And the Lord did so; and there came a grievous swarm of flies into the house of Pharaoh, and into his servants' houses, and into all the land of Egypt: the land was corrupted by reason of the swarm of flies. And Pharaoh called for Moses and for Aaron, and said, Go ye, sacrifice to your God in the land. And Moses said, It is not meet so to do; for we shall sacrifice the abomination of the Egyptians to the Lord our God: lo, shall we sacrifice the abomination of the Egyptians before their eyes, and will they not stone us? We will go three days' journey into the wilderness, and sacrifice to the Lord our God, as he shall command us. And Pharaoh said, I will let you go, that ye may sacrifice to the Lord your God in the wilderness; only ye shall not go very far away: intreat for me. And Moses said, Behold, I go out from thee, and I will intreat the Lord that the swarms of flies may depart from Pharaoh, from his servants, and from his people, to morrow: but let not Pharaoh deal deceitfully any more in not letting the people go to sacrifice to the Lord. And Moses went out from Pharaoh, and intreated the Lord. And the Lord did according to the word of Moses; and he removed the swarms of flies from Pharaoh, from his servants, and from his people; there remained not one. And Pharaoh hardened his heart at this time also, neither would he let the people go.

2. **Exodus 9:1-11** — Then the Lord said unto Moses, Go in unto Pharaoh, and tell him, Thus saith the Lord God of the Hebrews, Let my people go, that they may serve me. For if thou refuse to let them go, and wilt hold them still, Behold, the hand of the Lord is upon thy cattle which is in the field, upon the horses, upon the asses, upon the camels, upon the oxen, and upon the sheep: there shall be a very grievous murrain. And the Lord shall sever between the cattle of Israel and the cattle of Egypt: and there shall nothing die of all that is the children's of Israel. And the Lord appointed a set time, saying, To morrow the Lord shall do this thing in the land. And the Lord did that thing on the morrow, and all the cattle of Egypt died: but of the cattle of the children of Israel died not one. And Pharaoh sent, and, behold, there was not one of the cattle of the Israelites dead. And the heart of Pharaoh was hardened, and he did not let the people go. And the Lord said unto Moses and unto Aaron, Take to you handfuls of ashes of the furnace, and let Moses sprinkle it toward the heaven in the sight of Pharaoh. And it shall become small dust in all the land

of Egypt, and shall be a boil breaking forth with blains upon man, and upon beast, throughout all the land of Egypt. And they took ashes of the furnace, and stood before Pharaoh; and Moses sprinkled it up toward heaven; and it became a boil breaking forth with blains upon man, and upon beast. And the magicians could not stand before Moses because of the boils; for the boil was upon the magicians, and upon all the Egyptians.

GREEK WORDS

1. "swarm" — ground crawlers and insects; crocodiles, snakes, scorpions, other aggressive ground crawlers, and insects of every kind, including flies and caterpillars

SYNOPSIS

The children of Israel had been in bondage for more than 400 years. And their Egyptian taskmasters had beaten them into submission with rods, forcing them to perform extremely harsh labor. God heard the cries of His people and determined to deliver them and bring judgment upon the Egyptians for their abuse and cruel treatment of the Israelites. His judgment came in the form of ten plagues.

Have you ever thought, *Why plagues? Did they really happen? And was there any significance in the plagues that were unleashed?* The fact is, Israel really was enslaved in Egypt, and God really did bring judgment upon Pharaoh and the Egyptians. Each of the ten plagues was a direct assault on the gods of Egypt. God's primary purpose in bringing the plagues on Pharaoh and the Egyptians can be summed up in Exodus 12:12 (*NLT*): "…I will execute judgment against all the gods of Egypt, for I am the Lord!"

The emphasis of this lesson:

When the magicians recognized that the plague of lice was the finger of God, Pharaoh's heart was hardened. The Lord then sent three more plagues: swarms of flies; disease on the livestock in the field; and an outbreak of boils on both man and beast. Although these plagues devastated the Egyptians, the children of Israel remained safe and unharmed.

A REVIEW OF THE FIRST THREE PLAGUES

In our previous lesson, we examined the first three of the ten plagues God brought upon the land of Egypt. The **first plague** was *the waters of the Nile being turned into blood.* The Egyptians believed that the Nile was the birthplace of all the gods. By turning the waters to blood, God showed that He has complete power over…

- The god **Hapi** — who was believed to be the spirit of the Nile.
- The god **Khnum** — who was believed to be the guardian of the Nile.
- The god **Osiris** — who was believed to be the one who had the Nile as his bloodstream.

When the Nile River turned to blood, Hapi was humiliated; Khnum was shown to be incapable of providing protection; and Osiris seemed to have suffered a fatal wound and was bleeding profusely.

The **second plague** brought upon Egypt was *the massive invasion of frogs.* This was a direct assault on Heket, the Egyptian goddess of fertility whose head looked like a frog. It was almost as if God was saying, "You like to worship frogs? I'll give you frogs." And God caused the frogs to leave the waters and go into people's houses, bedrooms, beds, ovens, and even their cookware. Because frogs were a sacred symbol of the goddess Heket, the Egyptians wouldn't kill them.

The **third plague** God used to judge Egypt was turning the dust of the ground into *an infestation of lice.* This too was an attack on the false gods of the Egyptians who worshiped creeping things. It was also the first plague that the magicians of Egypt could not duplicate.

Plague #4: *God Sent 'Swarms' of Flies*

These 'Swarms' Were More Than Just Flies

When Pharaoh's heart was hardened and he refused to let the children of Israel go after the plague of the lice, the Bible says, "And the Lord said unto Moses, Rise up early in the morning, and stand before Pharaoh; lo, he cometh forth to the water; and say unto him, Thus saith the Lord, Let my people go, that they may serve me. Else, if thou wilt not let my people go, behold, I will send swarms of flies upon thee, and upon thy servants, and upon thy people, and into thy houses: and the houses of the Egyptians shall be full of swarms of flies, and also the ground whereon they are (Exodus 8:20,21).

What's very interesting about this passage is that the Hebrew word for "swarms" here implies *ground crawlers* and *insects*. This includes snakes, scorpions, crocodiles, other aggressive ground crawlers, and insects of every kind — such as flies and caterpillars (these include the devouring insects mentioned in Psalm 78). It appears that once this plague was announced to Pharaoh, God directed these types of animals and insects to attack the Egyptians.

Just as God summoned animals to Noah to go into the ark, now He was summoning all these creeping beasts out of their dens and hiding places in the earth and drawing them into Egypt. One Rabbi said that eventually the ground was teaming with crocodiles, snakes, scorpions, and creeping things. They were everywhere.

So "swarms of flies" was actually a plague of all kinds of creeping things with an emphasis on crocodiles. This was the equivalent of God striking the Egyptian god Sobek who was the crocodile god. And since the Egyptians worshiped crocodiles and creeping things, they considered them to be sacred and wouldn't kill any of these irritating invaders.

God's People Were Unaffected

God went on to say, "And I will sever in that day the land of Goshen, in which my people dwell, that no swarms of flies shall be there; to the end thou mayest know that I am the Lord in the midst of the earth. And I will put a division between my people and thy people: to morrow shall this sign be" (Exodus 8:22,23).

God made it clear to Pharaoh that He would keep the swarms from entering Goshen. These *ground crawlers* and *insects* would not hurt the Lord's people in any way. God wanted Pharaoh to know that there was something special about His people, the children of Israel. It's also important to note that God said He would bring this fourth plague "tomorrow." He could have brought it immediately, but by bringing it the next day, God was giving the Egyptians time to repent. At the same time, He was giving the animals time to leave their various habitats to come into Egypt.

Exodus 8:24 says, "And the Lord did so; and there came a grievous swarm of flies into the house of Pharaoh, and into his servants' houses, and into all the land of Egypt: the land was corrupted by reason of the swarm of flies." Eerily, animals slithered out from their underground dens onto the ground and began to encroach upon the people whom they naturally would have feared and avoided.

Psalm 78:45 says these swarms devoured them — indicating that there was a biting aspect to these swarms that attacked the Egyptians. Specifically, the Bible says a grievous swarm came into the house of Pharaoh, into his servants' houses, and into all the land of Egypt. Thus, no one was spared this terrible plague — except for the children of Israel in Goshen.

Indeed, "...The land was corrupted by reason of the swarm..." (Exodus 8:24). Ancient rabbis wrote that even babies were snatched from their cradles by these devouring animals. Again, this stopped the worship of Egyptian gods as they could not be worshiped in the midst of this uncleanness.

Pharaoh Said the Israelites Could Sacrifice to God in Egypt or Not Very Far Away

Scripture goes on to say, "And Pharaoh called for Moses and for Aaron, and said, Go ye, sacrifice to your God in the land" (Exodus 8:25). When the pressure of the plague ramped up, suddenly Pharaoh wanted to negotiate with Moses and the Lord. But he wanted Moses to stay in the land of Egypt and sacrifice to God. To this, "...Moses said, It is not meet so to do; for we shall sacrifice the abomination of the Egyptians to the Lord our God: lo, shall we sacrifice the abomination of the Egyptians before their eyes, and will they not stone us?" (Exodus 8:26,27)

To be clear: Egyptians didn't believe in shedding blood nor did they enjoy seeing it. This is why the Nile waters being turned to blood was such an abomination to them. One scholar says Moses refused on the grounds that to sacrifice in Egypt would be like killing a pig in a Muslim mosque or slaughtering a cow in a Hindu temple. The Egyptians would consider the sacrifice of a sacred animal to be blasphemous. Hence, Moses told Pharaoh, "We will go three days' journey into the wilderness, and sacrifice to the Lord our God, as he shall command us. And Pharaoh said, I will let you go, that ye may sacrifice to the Lord your God in the wilderness; only ye shall not go very far away: intreat for me" (Exodus 8:27,28).

In response, "…Moses said, Behold, I go out from thee, and I will intreat the Lord that the swarms of flies may depart from Pharaoh, from his servants, and from his people, to morrow: but let not Pharaoh deal deceitfully any more in not letting the people go to sacrifice to the Lord" (Exodus 8:29). The word "tomorrow" here tells us God gave the "swarms" time to retreat to where they had come from. Just as He summoned the swarms, now he would give them time to go back to where they came from.

Once the Swarm Was Removed Pharaoh's Heart Was Hardened

The Bible goes on to say, "And Moses went out from Pharaoh, and intreated the Lord. And the Lord did according to the word of Moses; and he removed the swarms of flies from Pharaoh, from his servants, and from his people; there remained not one" (Exodus 8:30, 31). Once again, after Moses prayed and the plague was lifted, we see that "…Pharaoh hardened his heart at this time also, neither would he let the people go" (Exodus 8:32).

Now, we do not know if Pharaoh deliberately lied to Moses or simply changed his mind once the "swarms" were gone. Many people turn to God in a time of calamity, and when things get better, they allow their hearts to become hard again. Whatever the case may be, we know that Pharaoh did not keep his word. Therefore, another plague was about to be unleashed on the inhabitants of the land.

Plague #5: *God Released Disease on the Livestock*

Only the Egyptians' Cattle Died — Not the Israelites' Cattle

Once more the Bible says, "Then the Lord said unto Moses, Go in unto Pharaoh, and tell him, Thus saith the Lord God of the Hebrews, Let my people go, that they may serve me" (Exodus 9:1). Notice the phrase "Go in unto Pharaoh." This implies that Moses and Aaron were to go into *Pharaoh's personal chambers*, which is what the Talmud indicates they had access to. Equally important here is the phrase "Tell him." This is a translation of a Hebrew word that implies *harsh talk*. In other words, Moses delivered this word from the Lord with urgency because this plague would be extremely devastating to the land of Egypt.

Moses continued by saying, "For if thou refuse to let them go, and wilt hold them still, Behold, the hand of the Lord is upon thy cattle which is in the field, upon the horses, upon the asses, upon the camels, upon the oxen, and upon the sheep: there shall be a very grievous murrain" (Exodus 9:2,3). Here again we see Pharaoh was given a warning that another plague was on the way. This one would severely damage the livestock of Egypt — specifically the animals in the field. This meant the animals in covered shelters would be spared.

To this Moses added, "And the Lord shall sever between the cattle of Israel and the cattle of Egypt: and there shall nothing die of all that is the children's of Israel" (Exodus 9:4). So just as with other plagues, this one would not affect God's people. Their livestock would be untouched. What's interesting is that history reveals that the Egyptians kept most of their animals out in the fields in the land of Goshen, side by side with livestock of the children of Israel. The ground there was fertile, and the fields were lush. Therefore, when this plague hit, the animals owned by the Egyptians would fall dead in the field, while standing next to the animals of the Israelites which would be unharmed.

When would this plague take place? The Bible says, "And the Lord appointed a set time, saying, To morrow the Lord shall do this thing in the land" (Exodus 9:5). Again, we see the plague was scheduled for "tomorrow." God was giving Pharaoh time to repent and thereby avoid this judgment. Likewise, God was giving the Egyptians time to use their heads — to respond to God's mercy and get their animals into shelter. But Pharaoh didn't repent, neither did the Egyptians heed God's warning.

Exodus 9:6 says, "And the Lord did that thing on the morrow, and all the cattle of Egypt died: but of the cattle of the children of Israel died not one." Imagine the scene: All the cattle of Egypt died, but none of the cattle of the children of Israel died. The cattle of the Israelites stayed on their feet grazing, while the Egyptians' cattle dropped dead all around them.

This fifth plague was an assault on the Egyptian god Hathor who was thought to be a mother goddess in the form of a cow — a symbol of fertility. Through this divine act, God showed that He was also mightier than this pagan god. Scripture says, "And Pharaoh sent, and, behold, there was not one of the cattle of the Israelites dead. And the heart of Pharaoh was hardened, and he did not let the people go" (Exodus 9:7).

Plague #6: *God Produced Boils Upon Man and Beast*

'Boils' Were a Painful, Swelling, Skin Inflammation

With Pharaoh's heart once again hardened in rebellion, God wasted no time in bringing about the sixth plague against the Egyptians. The Bible tells us, "And the Lord said unto Moses and unto Aaron, Take to you handfuls of ashes of the furnace, and let Moses sprinkle it toward the heaven in the sight of Pharaoh. And it shall become small dust in all the land of Egypt, and shall be a boil breaking forth with blains upon man, and upon beast, throughout all the land of Egypt" (Exodus 9:8,9).

To understand this verse, you need to know that the *furnace* mentioned here contained the ashes of the sacrifices that had been offered to the gods of Egypt. Essentially, God told Moses and Aaron to take the unholy soot from the pagan religious practices of the Egyptians and throw it in the air to be dispersed by the wind. Thus, the sacrifices to the gods the Egyptians adored would become a curse to them. Specifically, the dust would become "...a boil breaking forth with blains upon man, and upon beast, throughout all the land of Egypt" (Exodus 9:8,9). The word "blains" describes *blisters* or *boils* that were filled with a terrible fever or burning heat.

In obedience to God, Moses and Aaron "...took ashes of the furnace, and stood before Pharaoh; and Moses sprinkled it up toward heaven; and it became a boil breaking forth with blains upon man, and upon beast" (Exodus 9:10).

Again, these "blains" were *blisters* or *boils* that broke out in sores. The idea behind the ancient Hebrew word for "boil" is *to burn*. It carries the idea of *a swelling, painful, skin inflammation*. These painful blisters, boils, and sores affected people and animals. As we saw in an earlier lesson, the mummy of Thutmose II, which can be seen today in the Egyptian Museum, has boils and scars on it. This is the only Pharaoh to have such markings, which indicates Thutmose II is likely the Pharaoh who lived and ruled Egypt at the time of the Exodus.

The Bible goes on to say, "And the magicians could not stand before Moses because of the boils; for the boil was upon the magicians, and upon all the Egyptians" (Exodus 9:11). This plague was probably directed against the Egyptian god Imhotep, who was said to be the god of medicine. Even those closest to the Egyptian gods (the magicians) were stricken with this plague. This included the illustrious priests Jannes and Jambres. They were so covered with blisters, boils, and sores that they were embarrassed to be seen publicly.

Josephus wrote about this and said:

> But when Pharaoh did not even then yield to the will of God… God presently resolved to punish his wickedness with several sorts of calamities, and those worse than the foregoing, which yet had so generally afflicted them; for their bodies had terrible boils, breaking forth with blains, while they were already inwardly consumed; and a great part of the Egyptians perished in this manner.[1]

In our next lesson, we will focus on the seventh and eighth plagues God brought upon the land of Egypt — the plagues of *hail* and the *locusts.*

STUDY QUESTIONS

Study to shew thyself approved unto God, a workman that needeth not to be ashamed, rightly dividing the word of truth.
— 2 Timothy 2:15

1. The fourth plague God brought on the Egyptians is referred to in most English Bibles as "swarms of flies," but the words "of flies" don't appear in the original Hebrew text. What was most surprising and unexpected about the Hebrew meaning of the word "swarms"? How does this change the way you see this particular plague?
2. Two very interesting archaeological finds we have discovered so far in our study are:
   - There is an ancient stele (stone tablet or pillar) in the Museum of Cairo that documents that the children of Israel did actually reside in Egypt at one time.
   - The mummy of Thutmose II, which can be seen today in the Egyptian Museum in Cairo, has boils and scars on it. It is the only pharaonic remains with such markings.

   What do these facts say to you about the biblical narrative of the ten plagues and Israel's Exodus from Egypt? How do these facts strengthen your faith?

PRACTICAL APPLICATION

But be ye doers of the word, and not hearers only, deceiving your own selves.
—James 1:22

1. With many of the plagues, the Lord gave Pharaoh and the Egyptians a day's notice before it came. It was God's way of extending mercy and allowing time for them to repent. Can you remember a time when God gave you space to repent? Take a moment to briefly describe the situation. What took place and why are you grateful for God's mercy?
2. Unfortunately, once the swarms of flies were removed, Pharaoh changed his mind and didn't let the Israelites go free. Have you ever done that? Have you not kept your word once God pulled you out of trouble and things got better? What did you promise God you would do that you failed to follow through on? Take time now to *repent* and ask God to forgive you. Then take the steps you need to take to do what you said you were going to do.

---

[1] Flavius Josephus, "The Words of Flavius Josephus: Translated by William Whiston; Antiquities of the Jews," Book II, chap. 14.4.

LESSON 9

TOPIC

Plagues of Hail and Locusts

SCRIPTURES

1. **Exodus 9:13-15,18-35** — And the Lord said unto Moses, Rise up early in the morning, and stand before Pharaoh, and say unto him, Thus saith the Lord God of the Hebrews, Let my people go, that they may serve me. For I will at this time send all my plagues upon thine heart, and upon thy servants, and upon thy people; that thou mayest know that there is none like me in all the earth. For now I will stretch out my hand, that I may smite thee and thy people with pestilence; and thou shalt be cut off from the earth.... Behold, to

morrow about this time I will cause it to rain a very grievous hail, such as hath not been in Egypt since the foundation thereof even until now. Send therefore now, and gather thy cattle, and all that thou hast in the field; for upon every man and beast which shall be found in the field, and shall not be brought home, the hail shall come down upon them, and they shall die. He that feared the word of the Lord among the servants of Pharaoh made his servants and his cattle flee into the houses: And he that regarded not the word of the Lord left his servants and his cattle in the field. And the Lord said unto Moses, Stretch forth thine hand toward heaven, that there may be hail in all the land of Egypt, upon man, and upon beast, and upon every herb of the field, throughout the land of Egypt. And Moses stretched forth his rod toward heaven: and the Lord sent thunder and hail, and the fire ran along upon the ground; and the Lord rained hail upon the land of Egypt. So there was hail, and fire mingled with the hail, very grievous, such as there was none like it in all the land of Egypt since it became a nation. And the hail smote throughout all the land of Egypt all that was in the field, both man and beast; and the hail smote every herb of the field, and brake every tree of the field. Only in the land of Goshen, where the children of Israel were, was there no hail. And Pharaoh sent, and called for Moses and Aaron, and said unto them, I have sinned this time: the Lord is righteous, and I and my people are wicked. Intreat the Lord (for it is enough) that there be no more mighty thunderings and hail; and I will let you go, and ye shall stay no longer. And Moses said unto him, As soon as I am gone out of the city, I will spread abroad my hands unto the Lord; and the thunder shall cease, neither shall there be any more hail; that thou mayest know how that the earth is the Lord's. But as for thee and thy servants, I know that ye will not yet fear the Lord God. And the flax and the barley was smitten: for the barley was in the ear, and the flax was bolled. But the wheat and the rie were not smitten: for they were not grown up. And Moses went out of the city from Pharaoh, and spread abroad his hands unto the Lord: and the thunders and hail ceased, and the rain was not poured upon the earth. And when Pharaoh saw that the rain and the hail and the thunders were ceased, he sinned yet more, and hardened his heart, he and his servants. And the heart of Pharaoh was hardened, neither would he let the children of Israel go; as the Lord had spoken by Moses.

2. **Exodus 10:1-19** — And the Lord said unto Moses, Go in unto Pharaoh: for I have hardened his heart, and the heart of his servants, that I might shew these my signs before him: And that thou mayest tell in the ears of thy son, and of thy son's son, what things I have wrought in Egypt, and my signs which I have done among them; that ye may know how that I am the Lord. And Moses and Aaron came in unto Pharaoh, and said unto him, Thus saith the Lord God of the Hebrews, How long wilt thou refuse to humble thyself before me? let my people go, that they may serve me. Else, if thou refuse to let my people go, behold, to morrow will I bring the locusts into thy coast: And they shall cover the face of the earth, that one cannot be able to see the earth: and they shall eat the residue of that which is escaped, which remaineth unto you from the hail, and shall eat every tree which groweth for you out of the field: And they shall fill thy houses, and the houses of all thy servants, and the houses of all the Egyptians; which neither thy fathers, nor thy fathers' fathers have seen, since the day that they were upon the earth unto this day. And he turned himself, and went out from Pharaoh. And Pharaoh's servants said unto him, How long shall this man be a snare unto us? let the men go, that they may serve the Lord their God: knowest thou not yet that Egypt is destroyed? And Moses and Aaron were brought again unto Pharaoh: and he said unto them, Go, serve the Lord your God: but who are they that shall go? And Moses said, We will go with our young and with our old, with our sons and with our daughters, with our flocks and with our herds will we go; for we must hold a feast unto the Lord. And he said unto them, Let the Lord be so with you, as I will let you go, and your little ones: look to it; for evil is before you. Not so: go now ye that are men, and serve the Lord; for that ye did desire. And they were driven out from Pharaoh's presence. And the Lord said unto Moses, Stretch out thine hand over the land of Egypt for the locusts, that they may come up upon the land of Egypt, and eat every herb of the land, even all that the hail hath left. And Moses stretched forth his rod over the land of Egypt, and the Lord brought an east wind upon the land all that day, and all that night; and when it was morning, the east wind brought the locusts. And the locusts went up over all the land of Egypt, and rested in all the coasts of Egypt: very grievous were they; before them there were no such locusts as they, neither after them shall be such. For they covered the face of the whole earth, so that the land was darkened; and they did

eat every herb of the land, and all the fruit of the trees which the hail had left: and there remained not any green thing in the trees, or in the herbs of the field, through all the land of Egypt. Then Pharaoh called for Moses and Aaron in haste; and he said, I have sinned against the Lord your God, and against you. Now therefore forgive, I pray thee, my sin only this once, and intreat the Lord your God, that he may take away from me this death only. And he went out from Pharaoh, and intreated the Lord. And the Lord turned a mighty strong west wind, which took away the locusts, and cast them into the Red sea; there remained not one locust in all the coasts of Egypt.

GREEK WORDS

There are no Greek words for this lesson.

SYNOPSIS

When we think of the earliest civilizations in history, Egypt is most certainly at the top of the list. Today, thousands of years after it dominated the landscape of human existence, many of its major landmarks and cities can still be seen. Distinguished structures and places such as the ancient pyramids, the sphinx, the Valley of the Kings, and the temple ruins of Karnak, Luxor, and Kom Ombo all speak of Egypt's vast history and confirm the biblical accounts of the Old Testament — including the ten plagues that God brought against the land to set the nation of Israel free from captivity.

Because the Egyptians had brutally beaten the children of Israel for years and forced them into slavery, God used His mighty rod in the hand of His servant Moses to bring a just retribution against them. In fact, God went so far as to say to Pharaoh and the Egyptians, "...For this cause have I raised thee up, for to show in thee my power; and that my name may be declared throughout all the earth" (Exodus 9:16). Indeed, we serve a mighty God who does mighty things!

The emphasis of this lesson:

After the plague of boils, the Bible says the Lord hardened Pharaoh's heart. God then brought the most all-encompassing disaster on Egypt — the plague of thunderous, fiery hail. This was followed by an invasion

of locust, which devoured all that the hail had spared. According to Pharaoh's servants, the land of Egypt was now utterly destroyed.

A REVIEW OF THE FIRST SIX PLAGUES

The first sign God gave to Moses to display His power was to throw down his rod and it became a serpent. In ancient Egypt, the serpent — specifically the cobra — was a symbol of both power and protection for Pharaoh and his family. When Moses threw down his rod before Pharaoh and it became a serpent, the magicians of Egypt threw down their rods and they became serpents too. Yet, much to everyone's astonishment, Moses' rod (serpent) swallowed up all the rods (serpents) of the magicians! Through this demonstration, God declared to Pharaoh and all of Egypt, "I'm going to swallow up and devour all of your protection and power!" Friend, the gods of Egypt were no match for the One True God! He proved His might through the plagues He brought against the land.

PLAGUE #1: God Turned the Waters to BLOOD

The first plague God brought was to turn the waters of the Nile into blood. The Egyptians believed that the Nile was the birthplace of all the gods. By changing the waters to blood, God showed that He has complete power over...

- The god **Hapi** — who was believed to be the spirit of the Nile.
- The god **Khnum** — who was believed to be the guardian of the Nile.
- The god **Osiris** — who was believed to be the one who had the Nile as his bloodstream.

When the Nile River turned to blood, it became clear that Hapi had no real power over the Nile; Khnum was shown to be incapable of protecting the Nile; and Osiris seemed to be bleeding profusely from a lethal stabbing. God took down three Egyptian gods in this one plague!

PLAGUE #2: God Caused a Massive Invasion of FROGS

The second plague brought upon Egypt was the invasion of frogs. This was a direct strike on the Egyptian goddess Heket, the god of fertility, which looked like a frog. It was God's way of saying, "Since you like to worship frogs, I'll give you frogs." And God caused the frogs to leave the waters and come into people's houses, bedrooms, beds, ovens, and into their cookware. But because frogs were believed to be sacred, the Egyptians wouldn't kill them. Hence, they pleaded with Moses to remove them.

PLAGUE #3: God Created an Infestation of LICE

An infestation of lice was the third plague God used to judge Egypt. When Aaron struck the dust with Moses' rod, the dust became lice that clung to both men and beasts. This too was an attack on the false gods of the Egyptians who worshiped creeping things like lice. It was also the first wonder God performed that the magicians of Egypt could not duplicate.

PLAGUE #4: God Sent SWARMS of FLIES

Most English Bible versions say the fourth plague God brought was "swarms of flies." However, in the original Hebrew, the text simply says a "swarm." This word describes *ground crawlers* and *insects* and includes snakes, scorpions, crocodiles, other aggressive ground crawlers, and insects of every kind — such as flies and caterpillars.

Interestingly, the emphasis implied here in the word "swarms" is on *crocodiles*. This indicates that the fourth plague was a pointblank attack on the Egyptian god Sobek who was the crocodile god. And since the Egyptians worshiped crocodiles and creeping things, they considered them to be sacred and wouldn't kill any of these irritating and dangerous invaders. They were forced to tolerate this horrific plague until the God of all power retracted it and sent the "swarms" away.

PLAGUE #5: God Released DISEASE on the LIVESTOCK

The fifth plague that came upon Egypt was disease on all their livestock in the field. Supernaturally, all the cattle of Egypt died, but none of the cattle of the children of Israel died. The cattle of the Israelites stayed on their feet grazing, while the Egyptians' cattle dropped dead all around them. This plague was a head-on assault against the Egyptian god Hathor who was believed to be a fertility goddess that had the form of a cow.

PLAGUE #6: God Produced BOILS on Man and Beast

The sixth plague God brought upon Pharaoh and the Egyptians was boils that broke forth "...with blains upon man, and upon beast, throughout all the land of Egypt" (Exodus 9:9). The word "blains" describes *blisters* or *boils* that were filled with a terrible fever or burning heat. These boils affected everyone, including Pharaoh himself.

This plague was most likely directed against the Egyptian god Imhotep, who was said to be the god of medicine and healing. Even those closest to the Egyptian gods (the magicians) were stricken with this plague. This included Jannes and Jambres, the two chief Egyptian priests. They were so covered with blisters, boils, and sores that they were embarrassed to be seen publicly.

One by one, God struck down each of the Egyptian gods, proving to everyone that HE IS LORD and no one is greater!

Plague #7: *God Rained Fiery Hail*

This Plague and the Ones To Follow Would Be Most Severe

Amazingly, after six dreadful plagues pounded the people of Egypt, Pharaoh still would not relent and let the children of Israel go free. This moved God to unleash yet another plague. The Bible says, "And the Lord said unto Moses, Rise up early in the morning, and stand before Pharaoh, and say unto him, Thus saith the Lord God of the Hebrews, Let my people go, that they may serve me. For I will at this time send all my plagues upon thine heart, and upon thy servants, and upon thy people; that thou mayest know that there is none like me in all the earth" (Exodus 9:13,14).

There are two things we want to look at in this passage. First, note that God said to Pharaoh that He was going to send His plagues "upon thine heart." This indicates that what God was about to do was going to deeply touch Pharaoh in a very personal way. Also notice that God said, "I will send…all my plagues." This indicates that the plagues that were coming would be the worst of all the plagues so far.

Keep in mind that each plague was designed to answer Pharaoh's question, "…Who is the Lord, that I should obey his voice to let Israel go? (Exodus 5:2) Again and again, God was revealing who He is and proving that He is more powerful than every other god. Furthermore, each plague was also designed to give Pharaoh and Egypt an opportunity to repent and turn to God.

The Lord went on to say, "For now I will stretch out my hand, that I may smite thee and thy people with pestilence; and thou shalt be cut off from the earth" (Exodus 9:15). Remember, the Egyptians had placed taskmasters over the people of Israel who beat them with rods for decades — perhaps even for centuries. Now the tables were turned, and with the rod in Moses' hand, God was striking Egypt with all His might, letting them personally experience what it feels like to be beaten and afflicted.

Moses declared, "Behold, to morrow about this time I will cause it to rain a very grievous hail, such as hath not been in Egypt since the foundation thereof even until now" (Exodus 9:18). Again, we see the word "behold," which basically means, *Wow! What is coming is mind-boggling! You better get ready!*

This seventh plague would consist of thunder, rain, hail, and fire that would bring death to the surviving animals, crops, and the people who were exposed to it. And God qualified this plague saying it would be "such as hath not been in Egypt since the foundation thereof even until now" (Exodus 9:18). This implies it would be *like nothing that had ever occurred anywhere ever before.*

God Extended Mercy in the Midst of Judgment

When would the hail be coming? God said, "Tomorrow," once more offering Pharaoh and the Egyptians opportunity to repent.

In His mercy, God spoke to Pharaoh and the Egyptians through Moses saying, "Send therefore now, and gather thy cattle, and all that thou hast in the field; for upon every man and beast which shall be found in the field, and shall not be brought home, the hail shall come down upon them, and they shall die" (Exodus 9:19). Here again we see God's care of the animals as He urged Pharaoh and the Egyptians to protect their livestock. He knew every animal and person exposed would die in this plague. This hail would be so severe it would also have a damaging effect on buildings.

For the first time there were Egyptians that heeded God's word. Scripture says, "He that feared the word of the Lord among the servants of Pharaoh made his servants and his cattle flee into the houses: And he that regarded not the word of the Lord left his servants and his cattle in the field" (Exodus 9:20,21). This passage tells us there was a remnant among the Egyptians who finally began to acknowledge the God of Israel as greater than the gods of Egypt. This group was likely a part of the "mixed multitude" that left Egypt with the children of Israel during the Exodus (*see* Exodus 12:38).

The Damage From the Hail Was Devastating

The Bible goes on to say, "And the Lord said unto Moses, Stretch forth thine hand toward heaven, that there may be hail in all the land of Egypt, upon man, and upon beast, and upon every herb of the field, throughout the land of Egypt. And Moses stretched forth his rod toward heaven: and the Lord sent thunder and hail, and the fire ran along upon the ground; and the Lord rained hail upon the land of Egypt. So there was hail, and fire mingled with the hail, very grievous, such as there was none like it in all the land of Egypt since it became a nation" (Exodus 9:22-24).

Josephus spoke about this plague stating:

> ...Hail was sent down from heaven; and such hail it was, as the climate of Egypt had never suffered before, nor was it like to that which falls in other climates in winter time, but was larger than that which falls in the middle of spring to those that dwell in the northern, and north-western regions. This hail broke down their boughs laden with fruit....[1]

Clearly, no one had ever seen anything as frightening as this plague of hail. The Egyptians believed that the wrath of God was being poured down from Heaven. In addition to the enormous hail mingled with fire, there was also piercing thunder that was simply terrifying. It appears this plague was a direct attack on the Egyptian sky goddess Nut.

Scripture says, "And the hail smote throughout all the land of Egypt all that was in the field, both man and beast; and the hail smote every herb of the field, and brake every tree of the field. Only in the land of Goshen, where the children of Israel were, was there no hail" (Exodus 9:25,26). Once more, God made the distinction of who were His people, and He divinely protected them.

Pharaoh Pleaded for Moses' Help Then Hardened His Heart When the Hail Ended

In desperation, "...Pharaoh sent, and called for Moses and Aaron, and said unto them, I have sinned this time: the Lord is righteous, and I and my people are wicked. Intreat the Lord (for it is enough) that there be no more mighty thunderings and hail; and I will let you go, and ye shall stay no longer" (Exodus 9:27,28).

The reason Pharaoh "sent and called" for Moses to come to him was because he was petrified to go outside amidst the torrential hail and intense thunder. Ancient rabbis indicate that it was the terrifying thunder that gripped Pharaoh with fear more than anything else. Yet, Moses and Aaron were not afraid. They were divinely shielded from the fiery pounding of hail and thunder.

Responding to Pharaoh, "...Moses said unto him, As soon as I am gone out of the city, I will spread abroad my hands unto the Lord; and the thunder shall cease, neither shall there be any more hail; that thou mayest know how that the earth is the Lord's. But as for thee and thy servants, I know that ye will not yet fear the Lord God" (Exodus 9:29,30).

Based on previous experience, Moses knew Pharaoh would change his mind again. Nevertheless, irreparable damage had been done to Egypt. Scripture says, "And the flax and the barley was smitten: for the barley was in the ear, and the flax was bolled. But the wheat and the rie were not smitten: for they were not grown up" (Exodus 9:31,32).

The Bible goes on to say, "And Moses went out of the city from Pharaoh, and spread abroad his hands unto the Lord: and the thunders and hail ceased, and the rain was not poured upon the earth. And when Pharaoh saw that the rain and the hail and the thunders were ceased, he sinned yet more, and hardened his heart, he and his servants. And the heart of Pharaoh was hardened, neither would he let the children of Israel go; as the Lord had spoken by Moses" (Exodus 9:33-35).

Plague #8: *God Sent an Invasion of Locusts*

The Lord Was Making His Name Famous for Generations To Come

When we come to Exodus 10, we see that God spoke once again to Moses saying, "...Go in unto Pharaoh: for I have hardened his heart, and the heart of his servants, that I might shew these my signs before him: And that thou mayest tell in the ears of thy son, and of thy son's son, what things I have wrought in Egypt, and my signs which I have done among them; that ye may know how that I am the Lord" (Exodus 10:1,2).

This passage reveals that what God was doing through all these plagues was not only for the sake of the generation of Moses and Pharaoh. It was also for their "sons and their son's sons." God was looking forward into the future and making a mighty name for Himself for generations to come. He never wants us to forget the great things He has done in our lives. Therefore, we need to seize the opportunities we're given and tell our children and grandchildren about the wonderful ways God has provided for us and protected us. It will cultivate an attitude of gratitude and ignite a fire of faith in all who hear.

The Locusts Would Devour All That the Hail Spared

In obedience to God's instruction, the Bible says, "And Moses and Aaron came in unto Pharaoh, and said unto him, Thus saith the Lord God of the Hebrews, How long wilt thou refuse to humble thyself before me? let my people go, that they may serve me. Else, if thou refuse to let my people go, behold, to morrow will I bring the locusts into thy coast" (Exodus 10:3,4). Again, God gave Pharaoh and the Egyptians space to repent, warning that the next plague — a plague of locusts — would not be sent until *tomorrow*. This would also allow God time to bring the creatures from the east.

Regarding the locusts, Moses said, "And they shall cover the face of the earth, that one cannot be able to see the earth: and they shall eat the residue of that which is escaped, which remaineth unto you from the hail, and shall eat every tree which groweth for you out of the field: And they shall fill thy houses, and the houses of all thy servants, and the houses of all the Egyptians; which neither thy fathers, nor thy fathers' fathers have seen, since the day that they were upon the earth unto this day. And he turned himself, and went out from Pharaoh" (Exodus 10:5,6).

Pharaoh Put Limitations on Who He Would Allow To Leave Egypt

Of course, Pharaoh did not repent, but something was happening in the hearts and minds of his leaders. Exodus 10:7-9 says, "And Pharaoh's servants said unto him, How long shall this man be a snare unto us? let the men go, that they may serve the Lord their God: knowest thou not yet that Egypt is destroyed? And Moses and Aaron were brought again unto Pharaoh: and he said unto them, Go, serve the Lord your God: but who are they that shall go? And Moses said, We will go with our young and with our old, with our sons and with our daughters, with our flocks and with our herds will we go; for we must hold a feast unto the Lord."

Basically, Moses said, "All of us are going to go and worship God — from the youngest to the oldest — and all our animals and possessions are going with us." But Pharaoh was not in agreement. "And he said unto them, Let the Lord be so with you, as I will let you go, and your little ones: look to it; for evil is before you. Not so: go now ye that are men, and serve the Lord; for that ye did desire. And they were driven out from Pharaoh's presence" (Exodus 10:10,11).

If you read between the lines, you'll see that Pharaoh was only permitting all the *men* to go out to the wilderness and worship the Lord, but the women and children were to stay behind in Egypt. In his mind, this would guarantee the men would return, and his slave labor force would remain under his control. But Moses didn't entertain or accept Pharaoh's offer. The only way he would leave Egypt was with everyone and everything in tow. There would not be a return trip.

All Remaining Vegetation Was Consumed by the Locusts

After being driven from Pharaoh's presence, "...The Lord said unto Moses, Stretch out thine hand over the land of Egypt for the locusts, that they may come up upon the land of Egypt, and eat every herb of the land, even all that the hail hath left. And Moses stretched forth his rod over the land of Egypt, and the Lord brought an east wind upon the land all that day, and all that night; and when it was morning, the east wind brought the locusts" (Exodus 10:12,13).

It's important to note that this eighth plague was a direct assault against the Egyptian god Set who was believed to be the protector of the crops. Through this unprecedented event, God would powerfully demonstrate that He is the greatest, striking down Set and proving Set had no power to protect the crops.

From the breaking of dawn, the Bible says, "...The locusts went up over all the land of Egypt, and rested in all the coasts of Egypt: very grievous were they; before them there were no such locusts as they, neither after them shall be such. For they covered the face of the whole earth, so that the land was darkened; and they did eat every herb of the land, and all the fruit of the trees which the hail had left: and there remained not any green thing in the trees, or in the herbs of the field, through all the land of Egypt. Then Pharaoh called for Moses and Aaron in haste; and he said, I have sinned against the Lord your God, and against you. Now therefore forgive, I pray thee, my sin only this once, and intreat the Lord your God, that he may take away from me this death only" (Exodus 10:14-17).

Notice it says that Pharaoh called for Moses and Aaron *in haste*. The reason he sent for them so swiftly was because all the vegetation in Egypt was on the verge of extinction. It literally was being completely devoured before his very eyes. In a great panic, Pharaoh offered words of repentance, but as before, they would prove to be false and flimsy words spoken in the heat of the moment.

Just as Moses had done several times before, the Bible says, "…He went out from Pharaoh, and intreated the Lord. And the Lord turned a mighty strong west wind, which took away the locusts, and cast them into the Red sea; there remained not one locust in all the coasts of Egypt" (Exodus 10:18,19).

And what happened next? That's right! Scripture says, "But the Lord hardened Pharaoh's heart, so that he would not let the children of Israel go" (Exodus 10:20). There were two more plagues God would send on Pharaoh and the land of Egypt: the plague of darkness and the death of the firstborn of Egypt. We will examine these in our final lesson.

STUDY QUESTIONS

Study to shew thyself approved unto God, a workman that needeth not to be ashamed, rightly dividing the word of truth.
— 2 Timothy 2:15

1. *Hail* was the seventh plague God brought upon the land of Egypt, and it was more severe and devastating than any of the previous plagues. Take a few moments to reflect on all the climatic conditions that accompanied the hail. What did you learn about this plague that you had not seen before? How does this demonstrate and amplify God's power in your eyes?
2. According to Exodus 10:1 and 2, what was God's purpose in hardening Pharaoh's heart? And what was His ultimate purpose in the lives of Moses and the Israelites? What does this say to you about how and what God is doing in *your* life?
3. Carefully read these passages in the book of Psalms. What do they tell you about what God wants you to do with the memories of what He's

done in your life? Pray and ask the Holy Spirit to help you cultivate this powerful practice in your life and the life of your family.

- Psalm 77:11-15
- Psalm 111:2-4
- Psalm 145:1-7
- Deuteronomy 4:9

PRACTICAL APPLICATION

But be ye doers of the word, and not hearers only, deceiving your own selves.
—James 1:22

1. As you read through the narrative of the ten plagues, you'll notice that Pharaoh repeatedly asked Moses to "intreat the Lord" or *pray* and *intercede* to God on his behalf. Have you ever had people who were mistreating you ask you to pray for them when they were going through a rough time? How did you respond? What can you learn from Moses' example and implement in your own life?
2. Without question, Pharaoh was Moses' enemy and an enemy to the Hebrew nation. You, too, have enemies in your life who persecute and mistreat you. How does Jesus say you are to respond to your enemies in Matthew 5:38-42? How about in Matthew 5:43-48? (Also consider Proverbs 25:21,22; Romans 12:20,21; and Jesus' words in Luke 23:34.)

---

[1]Flavius Josephus, "The Words of Flavius Josephus: Translated by William Whiston; Antiquities of the Jews," Book II, chap. 14.4.

LESSON 10

TOPIC

Darkness and the Death of the Firstborn

SCRIPTURES

1. **Exodus 10:21-26,28,29** — And the Lord said unto Moses, Stretch out thine hand toward heaven, that there may be darkness over the land of Egypt, even darkness which may be felt. And Moses stretched forth his hand toward heaven; and there was a thick darkness in all the land of Egypt three days: They saw not one another, neither rose any from his place for three days: but all the children of Israel had light in their dwellings. And Pharaoh called unto Moses, and said, Go ye, serve the Lord; only let your flocks and your herds be stayed: let your little ones also go with you. And Moses said, Thou must give us also sacrifices and burnt offerings, that we may sacrifice unto the Lord our God. Our cattle also shall go with us; there shall not an hoof be left behind; for thereof must we take to serve the Lord our God; and we know not with what we must serve the Lord, until we come thither.... And Pharaoh said unto him, Get thee from me, take heed to thyself, see my face no more; for in that day thou seest my face thou shalt die. And Moses said, Thou hast spoken well, I will see thy face again no more.
2. **Exodus 11:1-7,9** — And the Lord said unto Moses, Yet will I bring one plague more upon Pharaoh, and upon Egypt; afterwards he will let you go hence: when he shall let you go, he shall surely thrust you out hence altogether. Speak now in the ears of the people, and let every man borrow of his neighbour, and every woman of her neighbour, jewels of silver, and jewels of gold. And the Lord gave the people favour in the sight of the Egyptians. Moreover the man Moses was very great in the land of Egypt, in the sight of Pharaoh's servants, and in the sight of the people. And Moses said, Thus saith the Lord, About midnight will I go out into the midst of Egypt: And all the firstborn in the land of Egypt shall die, from the firstborn of Pharaoh that sitteth upon his throne, even unto the firstborn of the maidser-

vant that is behind the mill; and all the firstborn of beasts. And there shall be a great cry throughout all the land of Egypt, such as there was none like it, nor shall be like it any more. But against any of the children of Israel shall not a dog move his tongue, against man or beast: that ye may know how that the Lord doth put a difference between the Egyptians and Israel.... And the Lord said unto Moses, Pharaoh shall not hearken unto you; that my wonders may be multiplied in the land of Egypt.

3. **Exodus 12:1,3,5-7,11-13** — And the Lord spake unto Moses and Aaron in the land of Egypt, saying... Speak ye unto all the congregation of Israel, saying, In the tenth day of this month they shall take to them every man a lamb, according to the house of their fathers, a lamb for an house.... Your lamb shall be without blemish, a male of the first year: ye shall take it out from the sheep, or from the goats: And ye shall keep it up until the fourteenth day of the same month: and the whole assembly of the congregation of Israel shall kill it in the evening. And they shall take of the blood, and strike it on the two side posts and on the upper door post of the houses, wherein they shall eat it.... And thus shall ye eat it; with your loins girded, your shoes on your feet, and your staff in your hand; and ye shall eat it in haste: it is the Lord's passover. For I will pass through the land of Egypt this night, and will smite all the firstborn in the land of Egypt, both man and beast; and against all the gods of Egypt I will execute judgment: I am the Lord. And the blood shall be to you for a token upon the houses where ye are: and when I see the blood, I will pass over you, and the plague shall not be upon you to destroy you, when I smite the land of Egypt.
4. **Exodus 12:21-23,28-29** — Then Moses called for all the elders of Israel, and said unto them, Draw out and take you a lamb according to your families, and kill the passover. And ye shall take a bunch of hyssop, and dip it in the blood that is in the bason, and strike the lintel and the two side posts with the blood that is in the bason; and none of you shall go out at the door of his house until the morning. For the Lord will pass through to smite the Egyptians; and when he seeth the blood upon the lintel, and on the two side posts, the Lord will pass over the door, and will not suffer the destroyer to come in unto your houses to smite you.... And the children of Israel went away, and did as the Lord had commanded Moses and Aaron, so did they. And it came to pass, that at midnight the Lord smote all the firstborn in the

land of Egypt, from the firstborn of Pharaoh that sat on his throne unto the firstborn of the captive that was in the dungeon; and all the firstborn of cattle.

5. **Exodus 12:30-31,33-38** — And Pharaoh rose up in the night, he, and all his servants, and all the Egyptians; and there was a great cry in Egypt; for there was not a house where there was not one dead. And he called for Moses and Aaron by night, and said, Rise up, and get you forth from among my people, both ye and the children of Israel; and go, serve the Lord, as ye have said.... And the Egyptians were urgent upon the people, that they might send them out of the land in haste; for they said, We be all dead men. And the people took their dough before it was leavened, their kneadingtroughs being bound up in their clothes upon their shoulders. And the children of Israel did according to the word of Moses; and they borrowed of the Egyptians jewels of silver, and jewels of gold, and raiment: And the Lord gave the people favour in the sight of the Egyptians, so that they lent unto them such things as they required. And they spoiled the Egyptians. And the children of Israel journeyed from Rameses to Succoth, about six hundred thousand on foot that were men, beside children. And a mixed multitude went up also with them; and flocks, and herds, even very much cattle.
6. **Exodus 12:41,51** — And it came to pass at the end of the four hundred and thirty years, even the selfsame day it came to pass, that all the hosts of the Lord went out from the land of Egypt.... And it came to pass the selfsame day, that the Lord did bring the children of Israel out of the land of Egypt....

GREEK WORDS

There are no Greek words in this lesson.

SYNOPSIS

If you were to take a voyage up the Nile River today, you would see the temples of Karnak and Luxor as well as the Valley of the Kings where dozens of pharaohs are entombed. As you sail further inland, you would pass Kom Ombo, which is the temple of the crocodile, and the beautiful temple at Edfu dedicated to the god Horus. Eventually you would come upon the city of Aswan, which is where Abraham and Sarah picked up the Egyptian servant girl Hagar. And according to Coptic church records, Aswan is also where Mary, Joseph, and Jesus stayed when they were being pursued by spies sent out by King Herod.

All these cities and the ancient structures and artifacts they contain verify with great credence the fact that the events found in the pages of Scripture really did take place. This includes the powerful account of Moses and the ten plagues, which God brought upon the land of Egypt. God delivered the children of Israel with His mighty hand, and He is still in the delivering business today! Like Moses and the Hebrew nation, if you will listen carefully and obey His instructions, He will walk you into freedom in every area of your life!

The emphasis of this lesson:

The ninth plague God sent on the land of Egypt was three days of darkness. This was followed by the ultimate plague, the death of the firstborn of all the Egyptians. As Israel applied the blood of the Passover lamb to their homes and stayed under its protection, they were kept safe from all harm. With this final blow, the Lord delivered Israel from captivity.

Through our previous lessons, we have seen how God in His unrivaled ability humiliated and defeated all the gods of Egypt. With each ensuing plague, a specific false god was targeted and taken down by God's power.

The FIRST PLAGUE — turning the waters into BLOOD — proved God is greater than…

- The Egyptian god **Hapi**, who was believed to be the *spirit of the Nile.*
- The Egyptian god **Khnum**, who was believed to be the *guardian of the Nile.*
- The Egyptian god **Osiris**, who was believed to have *the Nile as his bloodstream.*

The SECOND PLAGUE — a massive invasion of FROGS — proved God is greater than…

- The Egyptian goddess **Heket**, who was believed to be *the frog-goddess of fertility.*

The THIRD PLAGUE — an infestation of LICE — proved God is greater than…

- The Egyptian gods devoted to creeping things.

The FOURTH PLAGUE — swarms of FLIES — proved God is greater than…

- The Egyptian god **Sobek**, who was believed to be *the crocodile god.*

The FIFTH PLAGUE — DISEASE on the LIVESTOCK — proved God is greater than…

- The Egyptian goddess **Hathor**, a cow-like mother goddess who was believed to be *a god of fertility.*

The SIXTH PLAGUE — BOILS on men and beasts — proved God is greater than…

- The Egyptian god **Imhotep**, who was believed to be *the god of medicine and healing.*

The SEVENTH PLAGUE — thunderous HAIL mingled with fire — proved God is greater than…

- The Egyptian goddess **Nut**, who was believed to be *the sky goddess.*

The EIGHTH PLAGUE — an invasion of LOCUSTS — proved God is greater than…

- The Egyptian god **Set**, who was believed to be *the protector of the crops.*

What gods of Egypt would the final two plagues strike down? Let's dig into Scripture and find out.

Plague #9: *God Sent Three Days of Darkness*

Darkness Was a Direct Attack on Pharaoh and the Sun God Ra

After the locusts were removed by the strong west wind, Pharaoh's heart was once again hardened. "And the Lord said unto Moses, Stretch out thine hand toward heaven, that there may be darkness over the land of Egypt, even darkness which may be felt" (Exodus 10:21). This ninth plague — a plague of darkness — was not the normal darkness of night. It was a darkness that was so thick it could be felt. This plague would be a direct attack on two more Egyptian gods: the sun god Ra, and Pharaoh himself who was considered to be one of the children of the sun and god on earth.

The Bible says, "And Moses stretched forth his hand toward heaven; and there was a thick darkness in all the land of Egypt three days: They saw not one another, neither rose any from his place for three days: but all the children of Israel had light in their dwellings" (Exodus 10:22,23). Just as with previous plagues, God distinguished between the people of Egypt and His people, the children of Israel. When the Egyptians were paralyzed by darkness, the Hebrews living in Goshen were blessed to see the light of day.

Commenting on this ninth plague, Josephus wrote:

> ...A thick darkness, without the least light, spread itself over the Egyptians; whereby their sight being obstructed, and their breathing hindred by the thickness of the air, they died miserably; and under a terror lest they should be swallowed up by the dark cloud.[1]

The Bible then says, "And Pharaoh called unto Moses, and said, Go ye, serve the Lord; only let your flocks and your herds be stayed: let your little ones also go with you. And Moses said, Thou must give us also sacrifices and burnt offerings, that we may sacrifice unto the Lord our God. Our cattle also shall go with us; there shall not an hoof be left behind; for thereof must we take to serve the Lord our God; and we know not with what we must serve the Lord, until we come thither" (Exodus 10:24-26). Basically, Moses said, "When we go, we're taking everything and everyone with us."

Frustrated and infuriated, Pharaoh turned to Moses and said, "...Get thee from me, take heed to thyself, see my face no more; for in that day thou seest my face thou shalt die. And Moses said, Thou hast spoken well, I will see thy face again no more" (Exodus 10:28,29).

Plague #10: *The Death of the Firstborn*

God Gave the Israelites Great Favor

The tenth and final plague the Lord brought upon Pharaoh and the land of Egypt is recorded in Exodus 11 and 12. The Bible tells us, "And the Lord said unto Moses, Yet will I bring one plague more upon Pharaoh, and upon Egypt; afterwards he will let you go hence: when he shall let you go, he shall surely thrust you out hence altogether. Speak now in the ears of the people, and let every man borrow of his neighbour, and every woman of her neighbour, jewels of silver, and jewels of gold. And the Lord gave the people favour in the sight of the Egyptians. Moreover the man Moses was very great in the land of Egypt, in the sight of Pharaoh's servants, and in the sight of the people" (Exodus 11:1-3).

By this time the people of Egypt were exhausted and devastated by all the plagues. They were willing to give the Israelites gifts of silver and gold to persuade them to leave. God would see to it that Israel received full wages from their time in slavery and that they would not leave Egypt empty-handed. Moreover, Moses had become very great in the land of Egypt, in the sight of Pharaoh's servants, and in the sight of the people. They knew when Moses said something, it was going to happen.

This Final Plague Inflicted the Deepest Grief on Pharaoh and the Egyptians

Operating under the prophetic anointing of God, "...Moses said, Thus saith the Lord, About midnight will I go out into the midst of Egypt: And all the firstborn in the land of Egypt shall die, from the firstborn of Pharaoh that sitteth upon his throne, even unto the firstborn of the maidservant that is behind the mill; and all the firstborn of beasts" (Exodus 11:4,5).

This plague was quite unique in that God Himself would carry it out. He said, "I will go out." It would also be the most heart-wrenching plague of all as it would bring death to the firstborn of all humans and the firstborn of all animals in Egypt, and it would also affect Pharaoh's house.

Moses went on to say, "And there shall be a great cry throughout all the land of Egypt, such as there was none like it, nor shall be like it any more. But against any of the children of Israel shall not a dog move his tongue, against man or beast: that ye may know how that the Lord doth put a difference between the Egyptians and Israel" (Exodus 11:6,7).

This tenth plague — the death of every firstborn — would bring a weight of grief like Egypt had never before known. Yet, God's people — the children of Israel — would be insulated from death by an invisible barrier they themselves would be involved in establishing. One rabbi said, "But among the Israelites there was such tranquility that a dog would not have an occasion to even bark."

God, being infinite in knowledge, knew how Pharaoh would respond. Exodus 11:9 says, "And the Lord said unto Moses, Pharaoh shall not hearken unto you; that my wonders may be multiplied in the land of Egypt."

God's Establishment of Passover

A short time later, the Bible says, "And the Lord spake unto Moses and Aaron in the land of Egypt, saying... Speak ye unto all the congregation of Israel, saying, In the tenth day of this month they shall take to them every man a lamb, according to the house of their fathers, a lamb for an house... Your lamb shall be without blemish, a male of the first year: ye shall take it out from the sheep, or from the goats: And ye shall keep it up until the fourteenth day of the same month: and the whole assembly of the congregation of Israel shall kill it in the evening. And they shall take of the blood, and strike it on the two side posts and on the upper door post of the houses, wherein they shall eat it" (Exodus 12:1,3,5-7).

This lamb that was to be sacrificed was to be a young male without any defects or deformities. The blood of the lamb was to be applied to the doorway of the home — to the top beam and on each side of the doors. The lamb was then to be roasted and eaten together as a family (*see* Exodus 12:8-10).

Moses went on to say, "And thus shall ye eat it; with your loins girded, your shoes on your feet, and your staff in your hand; and ye shall eat it in haste: it is the Lord's passover" (Exodus 12:11). Notice the children of Israel were to eat the Passover lamb *in haste* — with their "loins girded, shoes on their feet, and their staff in hand." The reason for this hurried-up posture was because their deliverance was going to come very quickly, so they needed to be ready to move. Although they could not see their deliverance, they were to be ready for its arrival at a moment's notice. It would come quickly and they would all walk immediately out of Egypt.

This was the Lord's Passover. The word "Passover" means *to skip over* or *to pass over*. God literally *skipped* or *passed over* the homes whose doors were covered in the blood of the lamb. Here we see a powerful principle: **God does not judge where the blood is applied!** Thank God for the blood of Jesus that has been shed for us and applied to our lives!

Egypt's Firstborn Would Be Struck Down by God Himself

Speaking through Moses, God said, "For I will pass through the land of Egypt this night, and will smite all the firstborn in the land of Egypt, both man and beast; and against all the gods of Egypt I will execute judgment: I am the Lord" (Exodus 12:12). It is very important to understand that God regarded the nation of Israel as His *firstborn son*. In Exodus 4:22, He told Moses, "And thou shalt say unto Pharaoh, Thus saith the Lord, Israel is my son, even my firstborn." Because Egypt refused to release God's firstborn, God would now require the firstborn of Egypt.

God continued His instructions through Moses saying, "And the blood shall be to you for a token upon the houses where ye are: and when I see the blood, I will pass over you, and the plague shall not be upon you to destroy you, when I smite the land of Egypt" (Exodus 12:13). Again, this principle — **God does not judge where the blood is applied** — is so amazing, and it applies to us as believers. When God looks at us and sees the blood of Jesus applied to our lives, *His judgment for sin passes over us!* We are safe when we are *covered by the Blood*!

Moses Instructed the Elders of Israel How To Apply the Blood of the Passover Lamb

After the Lord had downloaded the blueprint for the Passover to Moses, "Then Moses called for all the elders of Israel, and said unto them, Draw out and take you a lamb according to your families, and kill the passover. And ye shall take a bunch of hyssop, and dip it in the blood that is in the bason, and strike the lintel and the two side posts with the blood that is in the bason; and none of you shall go out at the door of his house until the morning. For the Lord will pass through to smite the Egyptians; and when he seeth the blood upon the lintel, and on the two side posts, the Lord will pass over the door, and will not suffer the destroyer to come in unto your houses to smite you" (Exodus 12:21-23).

Once the blood of the Passover lamb had been applied to the three points of the doorway, all the Israelites were to stay behind the door and under the protection of the blood. The Lord was looking for the blood. The blood of the lamb was the requirement to be spared from judgment. After Moses gave these instructions, the Bible says, "And the children of Israel went away, and did as the Lord had commanded Moses and Aaron, so did they. And it came to pass, that at midnight the Lord smote all the firstborn in the land of Egypt, from the firstborn of Pharaoh that sat on his throne unto the firstborn of the captive that was in the dungeon; and all the firstborn of cattle" (Exodus 12:28,29).

In the End, Pharaoh Was Totally Humiliated

Just as with the nine plagues before it, this tenth plague was directed against two significant Egyptian gods. The first was *Osiris* — the Egyptian god who was believed to be the giver of life. The second god of Egypt targeted here was *Pharaoh* himself. Remember, Pharaoh was seen as a deity by all the Egyptians, and the fact that his own household was touched — that the firstborn of Pharaoh died — clearly demonstrated that the God of Israel was greater than Pharaoh.

Through this last plague, Pharaoh finally understood that the Lord God was greater than all the Egyptian gods — and was greater than Pharaoh himself. He was humiliated as his protection had been removed from him and his family line, just as it had been prophetically foreshadowed when Moses' rod turned into a serpent and swallowed up all the rods (serpents) of the Egyptian magicians.

The Bible says, "And Pharaoh rose up in the night, he, and all his servants, and all the Egyptians; and there was a great cry in Egypt; for there was not a house where there was not one dead" (Exodus 12:30). Remember, in Exodus 2:23, Israel *cried out* to God for deliverance from their harsh bondage. Now, Egypt *cried out* in deep anguish at the widespread loss of life in the land.

In the midst of great despair, the Bible says Pharaoh "…called for Moses and Aaron by night, and said, Rise up, and get you forth from among my people, both ye and the children of Israel; and go, serve the Lord, as ye have said" (Exodus 12:31). In other words, Pharaoh said, "Get up and get out — you and your whole clan!" This command to leave *immediately* is the reason God told the Israelites to be dressed, have their shoes on, and be ready to go.

Israel Left With the Spoils of Egypt

Scripture goes on to say, "And the Egyptians were urgent upon the people, that they might send them out of the land in haste; for they said, We be all dead men. And the people took their dough before it was leavened, their kneadingtroughs being bound up in their clothes upon their shoulders. And the children of Israel did according to the word of Moses; and they borrowed of the Egyptians jewels of silver, and jewels of gold, and raiment. And the Lord gave the people favour in the sight of the Egyptians, so that they lent unto them such things as they required. And they spoiled the Egyptians" (Exodus 12:33-36).

Regarding this final plague God brought upon the Egyptians, Josephus said:

> ...(By) one more plague he would compel the Egyptians to let Hebrews go... the destruction of the first-born... many of the Egyptians who lived near the King's palace, persuaded Pharaoh to let the Hebrews go. Accordingly he called for Moses, and bid them be gone; as supposing, that if once the Hebrews were gone out of the country, Egypt should be freed from its miseries. They also honored the Hebrews with gifts; some, in order to get them to depart quickly....[2]

Again, God is a God of justice, and He was making sure that the people of Israel were being reimbursed for all their labor in the land of Egypt.

It's interesting to note that when the aged Jacob entered Egypt during the years of famine — when Joseph was second in command — there were 70 "children of Israel" that settled in Goshen. How many departed from Egypt at the time of the Exodus? The Bible says, "And the children of Israel journeyed from Rameses to Succoth, about six hundred thousand on foot that were men, beside children" (Exodus 12:37).

Well, if there were about 600,000 men — and we add in women and children — it is safe to estimate that nearly 2,000,000 Hebrews left Egypt that day. And the Bible says, "And a mixed multitude went up also with them; and flocks, and herds, even very much cattle" (Exodus 12:38). As we have noted previously, this "mixed multitude" included a number of Egyptians who had repented of their actions and came to God as a result of all the plagues.

Amazingly, God had prophesied to Abraham more than four centuries earlier that his descendants would be *strangers in a land that was not their own* and be *afflicted four hundred years*. But God promised to deliver the Hebrews and bring them out with great substance (*see* Genesis 15:13,14).

In true form, the Bible says, "And it came to pass at the end of the four hundred and thirty years, even the selfsame day it came to pass, that all the hosts of the Lord went out from the land of Egypt. (Exodus12:41). And to drive home the fact that God keeps His promises, Exodus 12:51 says, "And it came to pass the selfsame day, that the Lord did bring the children of Israel out of the land of Egypt…."

Indeed, who is like the Lord! He is all-knowing! He is all-powerful! And He is the same yesterday, today, and forever! All praise and glory be to Him and Him alone!

STUDY QUESTIONS

Study to shew thyself approved unto God, a workman that needeth not to be ashamed, rightly dividing the word of truth.
— 2 Timothy 2:15

1. As God brought the ten plagues against Egypt, the Bible specifically says that He made a distinction between the Egyptians and the Israelites, His chosen people. Take a moment to look up the following verses and identify *how* God specifically demonstrated who were His own:
   - Exodus 8:22,23 ______________________________
   ____
   - Exodus 9:4,6______________________________
   ____
   - Exodus 9:26 ______________________________
   ____
   - Exodus 10:22,23______________________________
   ____
   - Exodus 11:7 ______________________________
   ____
   - Exodus 12:13______________________________
   ____

   Although the Bible doesn't specifically say what God did for Israel when He sent the plagues of blood, frogs, lice, boils, and the locusts, what do you think He did?

2. From the very beginning — when Moses was at Mount Horeb and God was first revealing to him the calling on his life — what did God tell Moses to say to Pharaoh about the nation of Israel? And what would the consequences be for Pharaoh's refusal to let the children of Israel go free? (*See* Exodus 4:21-23.) Why do you think God told Moses these things before he set foot back in Egypt?
3. The powerful principle demonstrated in the Passover story is that **God does not judge where the blood is applied!** How is the blood of Jesus different — and *greater* — than the blood of animals sacrificed in the Old Testament?

   - Hebrews 9:13,14 ____

     ____

   - Hebrews 10:3,4,11-14 ____

     ____

   - Hebrew 11:19-22 ____

     ____

PRACTICAL APPLICATION

But be ye doers of the word, and not hearers only, deceiving your own selves.
— James 1:22

1. As you complete this amazing study on Moses and the Ten Plagues, what is one of your greatest takeaways that you don't want to forget — something you are excited about and want to share with others?
2. The children of Israel were to eat the Passover lamb *in haste* — with their "loins girded, shoes on their feet, and their staff in hand." The reason for this hurried-up posture was because their deliverance was going to come very quickly. What has God spoken to you about your life? What has He promised to do? Are you ready to move and do what He said when the time comes? What adjustments do you need to make right now to be prepared?
3. In the Old Testament, the children of Israel were protected by the blood of the lamb on the doorposts of their homes. For us, we are protected by the blood of Jesus Christ applied to our very lives — He is our *Passover Lamb* (*see* 1 Corinthians 5:7). Although you cannot see or touch the blood of Jesus, you can symbolically apply His blood to

your life, to the lives of your family members, and to everything that concerns you. If you have not made this a practice, take time now to pray and cover yourself with the Blood! You can pray:

"Father, thank You for sending Jesus. Jesus, thank You for shedding Your blood for me. I cover myself and my family with the life-giving, sin-cleansing, devil-defeating blood of Jesus. I am saved and purchased by the Blood (Romans 5:9; 1 Peter 1:18,19). I apply the Blood to my mind, will, and emotions — declaring that my spirit, soul, and body are cleansed of all sin and guilt (Hebrews 9:14; 1 John 1:7,9). I apply the blood of Jesus to my home, my finances, my relationships, and my health. And I put the blood of Jesus against every demonic force coming against me (Revelation 12:11). Holy Spirit, remind me to apply the Blood each and every day. In Jesus' name. Amen!"

---

[1]Flavius Josephus, "The Words of Flavius Josephus: Translated by William Whiston; Antiquities of the Jews," Book II, chap. 14.5.

[2]Flavius Josephus, "The Words of Flavius Josephus: Translated by William Whiston; Antiquities of the Jews," Book II, chap. 14.6.

Notes

Notes

www.ingramcontent.com/pod-product-compliance
Lightning Source LLC
LaVergne TN
LVHW012334100826
845148LV00017B/2297

* 9 7 8 1 6 8 0 3 1 8 7 1 5 *